On the Smell of an Oily Rag

Speaking English, thinking Chinese and living Australian

Ouyang Yu came to Australia from Wuhan, China, in early 1991 and has since published 43 books of poetry, fiction, non-fiction, literary translation and criticism in English and Chinese languages. He also edits Australia's only Chinese literary journal, *Otherland* (since 1995). His noted books include his novel, *The Eastern Slope Chronicle* (2002), his collection of poetry, *Songs of the Last Chinese Poet* (1997), his translations in Chinese, *The Female Eunuch* (1991) and *The Man Who Loved Children* (1998), and his book of criticism, *Representing the Other: Chinese in Australian Fiction: 1888–1988* (forthcoming in the USA, 2008). He now writes and teaches part-time in China and Australia.

A select list of major publications by Ouyang Yu

Fiction in English

The Eastern Slope Chronicle (Brandl & Schlesinger Publishing, 2002), winner of the Festival Award for Innovation in Writing at the 2004 Adelaide Bank Festival of Arts.
Loose: a wild history (forthcoming with Bluechrome Publishing, UK, 2008)

Poetry in Chinese

Summer in Melbourne (Chongqing Publishing House, 1998)
xiandu (The Limit) (Otherland Publishing, Beijing, 2004)

Poetry in English

Moon over Melbourne and Other Poems (first published by Papyrus Publishing, 1995, new UK edition by Shearsman Books, London, 2005, new American edition by Rager Media, New York, 2008)
Songs of the Last Chinese Poet (Wild Peony Press, 1997)
New and Selected Poems by Ouyang Yu (Salt Publishing, UK, 2004)
The Kingsbury Tales: a novel (forthcoming with Brandl & Schlesinger, 2008)

Academic work in English

Representing the Other: Chinese in Australian Fiction: 1888–1988 (forthcoming in 2008 with Cambria Press, the USA)

Critical Work in Chinese

A History of Literary Exchange between China and Australia and between China and New Zealand (sole-edited and co-written by Ouyang Yu, forthcoming with Shandong Educational Publishing House, 2008)

Australian literature in Chinese translation

The Female Eunuch by Germaine Greer (Baihua Publishing House, 2002, first published in 1991 by Lijiang Publishing House, China)
The Ancestor Game by Alex Miller (Rye Field Publishing, Taiwan, 1996)
The Man Who Loved Children by Christina Stead (Chinese Literature Publishing House, 1999)
The Shock of the New by Robert Hughes (Baihua Publishing House, 2003)
Capricornia by Xavier Herbert (Chongqing Publishing House, 2004)

Chinese Literature in English Translation

In Your Face: Contemporary Chinese Poetry in English Translation, translated, edited and introduced by Ouyang Yu (Melbourne: Otherland Publishing, 2002)

English Fiction in Chinese translation

Corpsing by Toby Litt (Shanghai Literature and Arts Publishing House, 2006)

English Non-fiction in Chinese translation

The Story of English by Robert McCrum et al (Baihua Publishing House, 2004)

On the Smell of an Oily Rag

Speaking English, thinking Chinese and living Australian

Ouyang Yu

Wakefield Press

Wakefield Press
1 The Parade West
Kent Town
South Australia 5067
www.wakefieldpress.com.au

First published 2007

Edited by Bruce Sims
Cover and text designed by Liz Nicholson, DesignBITE
Typeset by Michael Deves, Lythrum Press
Printed and bound by Hyde Park Press

National Library of Australia
Cataloguing-in-publication entry

Author:	Ouyang, Yu, 1955– .
Title:	On the smell of an oily rag: speaking English, thinking Chinese and living Australian/author, Ouyang Yu.
Publisher:	Kent Town, S. Aust.: Wakefield Press, 2007.
ISBN:	978 1 86254 765 0 (pbk.):
Subjects:	Chinese language – Australia.
	English language – Australia.
	Chinese – Australia – Social life and customs.
	Literature, Comparative – Australian and Chinese.
	Literature, Comparative – Chinese and Australian.
	Intercultural communication – Australia.
	Cross-cultural studies – Australia.
Dewey Number:	305.7951094

Publication of this book was assisted by the Commonwealth Government through the Australia Council, its arts funding and advisory body.

For Chi, whose understanding of Chinese as a language and culture will hopefully improve through English.

Acknowledgement

This book has been many years in the making, since even before I became writer in residence at Peking University in 1999, with a grant from AsiaLink, for which I am grateful. There are many people I would like to thank: Bruce whose skilful editing brought the manuscript to fruition, Sandy whose active engagement with all relevant parties made it possible for the manuscript to be accepted for publication, and, of course, Michael for publishing it. Other people I'd like to thank are John and Stephen who read the manuscript in its earlier drafts and Mabel who read it in its final draft.

Permission is gratefully acknowledged from literary journals in which excerpts of this book have appeared, *Chelsea*, New York (No. 77, 2004, pp. 129–144); *Globalising Australia: Culture, Academia & Writing at the End of the Second Millennium*, A Meridian Book, Melbourne (February 2001, pp. 123–130), and *Heat*, Sydney (No. 9, 1998, pp. 137–148).

"Restless till death if the language doesn't amaze." DU FU

"Words close, meaning far." MENCIUS

"How long a time lies in one little word!" SHAKESPEARE

Contents

Introduction

China purchases a total of 50,000 titles annually from the West while the West only buys an appalling 2000 titles per annum from China. This lack of knowledge of or interest in Chinese language and culture can be remedied in some measure by this book.

Its contents are transient, a kind of linguistic orgasm, that moment of pleasurable explosion when you realise something new. Eastern Slope Su, the Chinese poet, described it succinctly about 900 years ago as like "moving clouds and flowing waters, of no fixed features, that move when they feel like moving and stop when they cannot but stop". It is writing that I intend to be enjoyable, but as fragmentary as when you switch between dozens of television channels.

In ancient China, there is a fiction called, *biji xiaoshuo* (roughly, pen-notes fiction), a fiction that contains disparate stories with no apparent interconnecting narrative, each on its own, each as short as a paragraph but no longer than a page. An exemplar is Ji Yun's *yuewei caotang biji* (Pen-notes at Yuewei Grass Hall) that runs to 541 pages. There is nothing comparable in Western fiction. Ji Yun's novel is postmodern by anticipating postmodernism by more than two hundred years. In fact, what is pre-modern in classical Chinese literature is like the postmodern in general Western literature, without its pretensions.

Based on this unique *biji* genre and written in an accessible, readable and deliberately un-academic style, *On the Smell of an Oily Rag* is a seminal non-fictional book that creates its own genre of what I call, *biji feixiaoshuo* (pen-notes non-fiction), in its exploration of cultural, linguistic and literary similarities, differences and parallels between the English and the Chinese languages in a distinctly Australian context. It draws references from a range of literary and cultural works going as far back as *The Book of Songs* (1122–256 BC).

For years, living and writing in Australia and imaginary China or vice versa as I am, I have never ceased to be amazed by the brilliant sparks that rub off at language contact points, creating a new language. This book grew out of a single spark ignited by the comparison between the Chinese and English languages in the expression, *san si*, on third thoughts, think thrice or triple thinking, compared with the English expression, on second thoughts, think twice or double thinking. It has now expanded to include sections on other aspects of the languages such as poetic mathematics, reversals, parallels, landscape, sounds, naming, similarities, illogicalities and untranslatabilities in relation to literature and culture, with a blending of various genres of diary, fiction, non-fiction, essay, translation and poetry.

Things sprout up spontaneously, in my readings of literatures of various countries, over centuries, ranging from Australia,

USA, UK, France, Germany, and, of course, China, in my multi-million character or word translations, both literary and commercial, of works written in English and Chinese, and in my literary sorties into many different genres of literature, including poetry, fiction, essays, literary criticism, literary magazine publishing, literary editing, again in English and Chinese. Ideas come to me at odd moments and in odd places: on the toilet bowl, in my bed, before my mind drifts into a dream at night or out of a dream in the morning, on board a trans-Pacific airline to San Francisco, driving home from the County Court in Melbourne after a long day's work interpreting, over dinner with friends from China or reading weekly English or Chinese newspapers in my backyard, my shoulders bathed in sunlight. It is a unique experience that has yet to find a match in the rest of the English or Chinese speaking world. Australia's quirky, maddening quietness has given me wild pleasure in playing bilingual games and has offered me rare gems embedded in the two languages, hidden from the view of even the most pedantic linguist in the world, so that I push the limits of English till I cross over into Chinese.

Writing like this is far from easy. The book has been in the making since mid-1998. Initially, it took a diary form. Gradually, it grew into a solid piece of writing, even in its quicksilver liquidity. To this day, I am still left with a feeling that the book is somehow growing and expanding like a dictionary, as my agent Sandy put it, like a natural and spontaneous growth, as I put it, and an East-West fusion to the degree of *ni zhong you wo, wo zhong you ni* (you in me, me in you), to borrow a Chinese saying. You can't hurry it through; you can't even edit it or bend it like Beckham; you have to live with it, like a tree, an organic thing, something that Westerners have only recently realised to be of vital importance but Chinese have been living with for the last few millennia, only to temporarily lose it at present as a result of massive Westernisation.

I have lately been thinking of the significant difference between the Chinese culture and the English culture in the word combination "nation-state", an abstract idea I can never relate to. In Chinese, we would have to say "nation-family" (*guo jia*), *guo* for nation and *jia* for family, a political term never gone out of currency. Furthermore, every Chinese learner of English knows that when he or she learns the English equivalent to the Chinese *guo jia*, he or she has to learn at least three words: nation, state and country, which are embodied in the single Chinese word, *guo*, a square character with four strokes on four sides serving as four boundaries, enclosing a smaller character, *yu* (jade), in its present simplified form or, two smaller characters, *kou* (mouth) and *ge* (dagger-axe, an ancient weapon) in the traditional script. So much for this character analysis and let me quickly come to my conclusion: the learning of English is the beginning of the dismantling process of the Chinese (character) as the notion of nation-family breaks up and down, giving way to that of nation-state and that of nation-state-country. The very reason why Bei Dao, Yang Lian and a host of other Chinese poets keep writing Chinese poetry despite living overseas for many years is perhaps their resistance to allow any languages, including English, to break their character apart.

The book also has a bibliography for interested researchers and linguists to further explore the subject.

I hope that this work will give pleasure and, for my part, I'll be pleased if you could benefit from my humble offering.

Ouyang Yu

1

Very Big, China

(Noel Coward)

Years ago, I found that the Chinese have a tendency to exaggerate things compared with their Western counterparts. In its simplest form, it can be by only one digit. Take "on second thoughts". In Chinese we go one step further by saying *san si*, "third thoughts", as in the proverb, "walk after third thoughts".

I was watching television today when I heard someone say "think twice" and, as if on cue, I was immediately taken to second thoughts, then third thoughts, and, finally, "think thrice", thus solving a problem long unresolved with the Chinese proverb "look before you leap" for *san si er hou xing*. Which now can be effortlessly and meaningfully translated as "think thrice before you walk". The more I dwell upon this, the more is revealed to me about the difference between the English addiction to the figure 2 and the Chinese addiction to the figure 3. In English, there are "on 2nd thoughts", "think twice", "a twice-told tale", "no 2nd chance", even "2nd guess", and in Chinese there are "3rd thoughts" or "think thrice"; *shi bu guo san* (not doing something for a third time); *zai san zai si* (again three again four), over and over again; and *san fan wu ci* (three occasions and five times), many times. Perhaps the English "Two's company, three's a crowd" can best help explain their dislike for the figure 3? But then the Chinese have a similar expression that goes, *yi ge he shang tiao shui chi, liang ge he shang tai shui chi, san ge he shang mei shui chi* (one monk shoulder-poles water to eat [to drink]; two monks carry water to eat and three monks have no water to eat).

I was just about to wrap up on this 2nd and 3rd thoughts business when I came across yet another instance of English or Australian addiction to 2, this time in a poem. In "After the moon walk" by Kathryn Lomer, a line goes, "I howl/twice at a moon ..." Well, if I wrote the poem, I might instinctively have written "I howl/thrice at a moon."

"Win-win" as in a win-win situation is translated into Chinese as "double-win" (*shuang ying*) and the inventive Chinese even go as far as "triple-win", which in English would have to be win-win-win, wouldn't it?

In numbers, Chinese as a language will always outstrip English by one digit, as in *luan qi ba zao* (at sevens and eights) and *wu ti tou di* (on all fives), this one a gesture of respect and admiration, with both knees, both elbows and the forehead on the ground.

In some extreme cases, the Chinese beat the English not just by one digit but by 998 digits. In late April 2003, I went to

Canberra on a research trip. While I made sure that I brought everything with me, clothes and books, even a porn DVD, I forgot one essential, my electric shaver. Stroking the quickly sprouted beard on my chin, I thought of this Chinese proverb, *zhi zhe qian lü, bi you yi shi; yu zhe qian lü, bi you yi de* (a wise man makes errors just as a dimwitted man makes gains). However, if translated word for word, "thousand thoughts" would emerge as *qian lü* (thousand thoughts or worries) meaning exactly that: even if a wise man thinks a thousand thoughts he is still prone to commit a mistake but if a dimwitted man thinks a thousand thoughts he may likely make a gain.

If language is an indication of national character, this mathematical sense of superiority still raises its head. In late June 2004, I went to Shenzhen and visited a business friend of mine. When I casually mentioned that I had been to Hamburg, one of the largest harbours in the world, he dismissed it by saying that Shenzhen Harbour was being developed into a bigger one. Then he added that in China they were always doing things faster, better and larger than "them".

Big. I know being big or wanting to be big is a *big* problem with the Chinese and their culture. In a recent issue of *Overland*, a poem talks about Americans' obsession with bigness, "Americans always brag that everything they have is bigger, better than the rest of the world. Their cars are bigger, their planes bigger, their trains bigger and their planes are bigger because they have to be bigger ..." Interestingly, I read an excellent article by Liu Xiaobo in a recent issue of *Ming Po Monthly*, in which he says, in my translation, "There is a deeply ingrained *da hua* (big word) tradition in the Chinese language, using big words to sing in high tones, to speak of great achievements, to praise saints, to be lyrical, to exaggerate and flatter with vanity ..."

Vivid examples of exaggeration come to mind straight away: *shi wan da shan* (one hundred thousand big mountains), the region around Guilin that I heard people mention when I went there in July 2004, and "My 5000 star hotel" as an Australian friend emailed me some years back to describe his holiday in the Outback.

"Dressed to the nines", I know, but the Chinese say *shi san fen* (the thirteens). Hence my new expression: dressed to the thirteens!

The Chinese have an exceptional mathematical brain, which can be seen from the number of awards they win in the annual International Olympic Mathematics Competition. Not surprisingly, this mathematical concern is prevalent in their language. Take a look at these examples: *yi qiong er bai* (one poor two blanks) for being poor and devoid of anything; *yi dao liang duan* (one knife two broken pieces) for severing at one blow and *yi mu shi hang* (one glance ten lines) for taking in ten lines at one glance. We like the numbers so much that we even translate the English "seeing is believing" into "hearing a hundred times is not as good as seeing it once" (*bai wen bu ru yi jian*). The extreme example is, of course, *wan sui* (ten thousand years), reserved for emperors and Mao, dwarfing the English "long live so and so". When Chinese shouted, I one of them, back in the 1960s, "Ten thousand years Chairman Mao" (Long Live Chairman Mao), were we all lying or were we only repeating a tradition of linguistic exaggeration that to this day still makes others, like the English, suspicious of our honesty and helps keep the stereotype alive?

One wonders how mathematics could find its way into poetry but that is something that ancient Chinese poets have been practising for centuries. At one stage in my life in Australia (seven years after my arrival in 1991), I grew pretty bored by the stuff written by white men and women. For a change, I took up reading ancient Chinese essays. My eyes lit up when I came across a mathematical reference in an essay by Yuan Hongdao, a Ming essayist and poet, in his description of Dongting Lake. He says, "The colours of the mountains are seventy-two and the lights of the lake are three thousand and six hundred." I can't help but remember all the poetic mathematics that I have come across before. Li Bai has two lines that run, "My white hair is three thousand *zhang* (one *zhang* is 3 1/3 metres) long/and the sorrow at departure travels the whole length of me." In another famous poem of his about the hard journey he made in Sichuan, he says, "It took forty-eight thousand years for people to go to the frontier fortress of Qin." An old man in the Song Dynasty was fishing in the moonlight and was singing to himself, "There are so many multiplications and divisions in the world but none is better than when I pull up my fishing line under the bright moon on a beautiful night," implying that if you divide what you multiply, it then equals zero. Jiang Tan, in his *Fragments Remembered under an Autumnal Lamp*, portrays a tea-making scene, in which he says that cooking tea over a bamboo stove is like receiving water sprinkling from the Buddha that "saturates his eighty-four thousand pores". Even Ouyang Xiu gave himself a title, "Six One Lay Buddhist", as he lives daily among his books, epigraphs, a zither, a chessboard and a bottle of wine, moving constantly among these five. One wonders why five. Ouyang Xiu said: an old man among five. That's why.

Chinese culture is such an exaggerated or exaggerating one that, in the published Chinese version of *Le dictionnaire khazar* by the Serbian writer Milorad Pavic, a relative is described as so distant that you can't reach him even if you strike out eight times with your pole – but I'm pretty sure this is not what Milorad says in the original Serbian version as it sounds so much like the original Chinese expression.

Somewhere, I think it's in Robert Hughes' *The Shock of the New*, I saw this: "meanings missed by a country mile". Do we not have a similar measuring system for meanings in Chinese? Yes, and with more exaggeration. See this: *cha zhi hao li, shi zhi qian li* (if you miss it here by a millimetre, you'll miss it there by thousands of *li*, one *li* being half a kilometre).

When we took our son to go to a private school, our main concern was the prevalent drug abuse among public school children that might have a bad influence on him. The school principal assured us that they would not allow such things to happen in their school. "If we find anyone taking drugs, that's it. He'll have to leave. There will be no second chance," she said. The equivalent Chinese expression is *xia bu wei li* (not again next time), which implies that the culprit could be forgiven the first time but would not be given a third chance, echoing another ancient Chinese expression *shi bu guo san* (not doing something bad for a third time). Thus, you see, a culture with a longer history is both more tolerant and more considerate, as shown by the additional digit.

When watching the film *The Grizzly Bear* I got a fragment of the conversation that goes, "If they're here in the boat, you'll be in seventh heaven." Although I have lost the context, I got what I wanted, the "seventh heaven", because that sounds very much like the Chinese expression *jiu chong tian* or "the ninth heaven." Now this is a case of us beating them again, by two digits! If the Chinese seem more tolerant than their Australian counterparts in allowing people more chances to make mistakes, then their concept of heaven and hell are also numerically superior, as shown in the expression "the ninth heaven" and "the eighteenth hell" (*shi ba ceng di yu*).

In Chinese, the figure 9 often means numerous. For example, if a road has too many twists and turns, you describe it as *san wan jiu zhuan* (three twists nine turns), and you refer to the sky as *jiu tian*, ninth heaven, to convey the extreme height of the sky. I suspect this figure also means similar things in English or else why do they say they are "walking on cloud nine" when they express their extreme delight at something?

I can never find anything quite the match for "keeping one's ears to the ground" until I hit the Chinese *yan guan liu lu, er ting ba fang* (the eye is watching the six roads and the ears are listening to the eight directions). Certainly, mathematics again plays an important role here.

Although English speakers are as like-minded as Chinese ones, they do seem more laconic. Take "in two minds". The closest Chinese comes to it is the expression, "in three hearts and two minds" (*san xin er yi*). "In three hearts and two minds" might make a good title, you never know.

Written more than two thousand years ago in one of *The Nineteen Ancient Poems in China*, the saying "A man lives a life shorter than a hundred years but worries a worry a thousand years long" still applies, both in reality and mathematically.

2

Double Trouble

(Stevie Ray Vaughan's Band)

In English when you refer to the head of an organisation, you refer to the head. The Chinese say it twice: *tou tou* (head head).

Mathematically, the Chinese language gains in the number of characters while its English counterpart grows less, which is what, as a rule, happens with translation: you translate into more Chinese characters than if you translate back into English words. You say "bye" but we say "bye-bye". You say, "Let me think"; we say, "Let me *xiang xiang* (thinkthink)."

I think I have finally worked this out today when I wrote *xiang xiang* (think think) in my article for a Chinese newspaper column. If I translate that particular expression into English,

I'd use "on second thoughts", both matching in their mathematics and their meaning.

I was ordering a lunchtime ravioli at Deakin University the other day when the assistant asked: "You like it hot as against cold, not hot as chilly hot?" Interesting question from a Chinese point of view because, when you come to think of it, Chinese have two different words for the first "hot" (*re*) and the second "hot" (*la*). If something is so hot that it generates heat in you, it is *re la la* (hot la-hot, la-hot). In English, you'd have to say it three times: hot hot hot.

A recent term for beautiful young women frequently found online is a Chinese word, *mei mei*, beautiful brow, a coinage based on, I suspect, *mei mei* for sisters or beautiful sisters, sometimes shortened as MM.

Someone was making a point about the universities not imposing restrictions on overseas students as possible terrorists when he said that the universities should not become "grand nannies". Now, that sounds very similar to a Chinese ear, such as mine, to the Chinese expression *po po ma ma*, grand nannies and mums. How to use it? Easy. If my wife is too fussy about things, I'll simply say: Don't be *po po ma ma*. She can say the same thing to me if I become fussy.

I was reading a Chinese book about gluttons in China when I came across an adverb that shed light on possible Chinese-Aboriginal connections. That is "wind wind fire fire" as in the sentence: "She went to the meat stand wind wind fire fire", which actually translates into "she went to the meat stand in a great hurry." What I mean is this reduplication in Chinese is exactly the same as the Aboriginal way of reduplicating, as in "Wagga Wagga", "Woy Woy", "Never-Never" and "devil-devil" or "debil-debil", a linguistic phenomenon that abounds in Chinese language: *shan shan shui shui* (mountain mountain water

water), *san san liang liang* (three three two two or in twos or threes), and *qian qian wan wan* (thousand thousand ten thousands ten thousands or numerous), just to cite a few of many such examples.

In assisting the police with robbery cases here in Australia, I came to notice that the word "steal" was not exactly what the Chinese word *tou* meant as the police sometimes refer to people taking things in front of the shop-owner as an act of stealing whereas in Chinese an act of *tou* would not occur in the presence of others or else it would be called *qiang* or robbing. In Chinese *tou* (steal) is always associated with *mo* (grope) as shown in such expressions as *tou tou mo mo* (steal steal grope grope) and *tou ji mo gou* (steal chickens and grope dogs), minor acts of theft.

In English you say "far exceeding" and in Chinese we say *yuan yuan chao guo* (far far exceeding). It is this that makes me wonder if our minds will never be entirely turned into yours or vice versa.

I did a job in the police station this afternoon and one of the interviewing officers referred to the interviewee as one of the "dodgiest" he'd ever met. The word "dodgy" immediately put me in mind of a Chinese word *duo* which sounds the same as the first part of the word "dodgy" and forms part of the word-combination, *duo duo shan shan,* meaning "dodgy dodgy", if you like.

3

Unexpected Reversals

(Robert Stone)

I recently read Zoe King: "... what looks superficially like the 'fresh and new' in writing is often that from other cultures, other countries, that we simply haven't met before." I wondered if this woman realised that in Chinese we don't say "fresh and new" but "new and fresh" or "new fresh" (*xin xian*)?

I saw this and just took it down, "embroidered birds and flowers", because in Chinese the order is *hua niao* (flowers and birds or flowers birds).

In *Capricornia,* Norman accused Mr Hollower of "living on the fat of the land", which won't easily translate into Chinese but there is something quite similar to it in Chinese except in reverse. In English, it roughly means "living on the fat of the people" (*sou gua min zi ming ao*).

You say dead tired but we say *lei si le* (tired dead).

In English you say "half-seriously" but in Chinese you say "half-jokingly", to mean the same thing.

You say "daybreak" but we say *po xiao* (break day or, to be more exact, break dawn).

I don't know why but sometimes there seems a wilfulness on the part of the Chinese to twist the meaning of English expressions around. Just one instance: where you say "storm in a teacup", the Chinese or Hong Kongese say *feng bo li de cha bei* (teacup in a storm), as the title of a television program in Hong Kong demonstrates.

In English you say "the mother-fucker". In Chinese we say "Fuck your mother's."

"Organised crime" pops up frequently in Germaine Greer's *The Whole Woman* which I translated and I have had no difficulty turning it into Chinese except in reverse, knowing that is the only way. In Chinese, it is *fan zui zu zhi* (criminal organisation).

The Chinese word *fan yi* (translation), consists of the word *fan*, which means to "turn" as in turning a new leaf or turning the corner. I often have the feeling that it is rather the other way around. It's not the *fan* for turning but the *fan* for reversing, pronounced exactly the same but on the third tone. When we say "Mum and Dad" in English, naturally enough, they say exactly the opposite in Chinese, "Dad and Mum" (*bama or baba mama*), also naturally enough. There are many other similar examples, which I shall have to skip here but one I came across recently while translating *Capricornia* reminds me again of this process of reversal. The word is "foot-and-mouth" disease, mentioned in a place when there is a boom in the cattle industry in *Capricornia*.

Hesitant to put it into Chinese the same way as it appears in English, I checked my dictionary, which gave me the definition in the opposite order: *kou ti yi* (mouth [and] foot disease)!

In English you say "a pleasant surprise" just as you would say *jing xi* in Chinese. It means the same, but reversely, "surprise pleasant."

Same with Coca Cola. You drink a Coke but a Chinese drinks a Cola (*kele*).

While "feel no pain" may describe the state of drunkenness, the Chinese have an expression about drinking that is just the opposite, *tong yin* (pain or painful drinking), which means drinking joyfully or to one's heart's content.

I have been wondering about the salt-based race and the sugar-based race since I got up this morning. One remark made by a friend of mine in Denmark last April forms the basis of this speculation. In the train station, over breakfast, he revealed that what he had missed most in China was sweet food at breakfast. That revelation caused me to comment that it was exactly the opposite that I missed in Australia: salty breakfasts with pickled vegetables. A race, I wonder, brought up on sugar-based food, must be in some essential way different from one raised on salt-based food, the former perhaps prone to creating a literature rich in sugar but lacking in salt, like their food.

The English stomach and the Chinese *du* (stomach or belly) have something in common, both a symbol of tolerance but the former more of intolerance (I can't stomach it) than the latter (*du da neng rong tian xia shi*), a description of Buddha who has such a big belly that he can tolerate everything under heaven!

When I met Professor Wang, a lexicographer at Suzhou University, in 1999, I raised the issue of reversal in English and Chinese. He pointed out that this is often the problem when cultures are translated into each other. For example, the camera referred to as "fool proof" is *sha gua ji*, "the fool's camera", in Chinese. The so-called "cheongsam" for woman with a slit opening on the side actually meant "long gown", the daily dress for Chinese men in the old days. And the "answering machine" is translated in Chinese as *lu yin dian hua*, "the recording telephone", with an opposite function to that of the answering machine.

I have noticed that you can play with the English words or expressions back and forth, such as "live", which is evil in reverse, and the expression, "when the going gets tough, the tough get going" as well as the expression, "you can take a Chinese out of China but you can't take China out of a Chinese". In Chinese, you can do the same to nearly all the character-combinations, such as *se qing* (sexy sentiments or pornography) and *qing se* (basically the same thing but deemed less offensive), and *bu pa yi wan, jiu pa wan yi* (one is not afraid of ten thousand, *yi wan*, but afraid of any eventualities, *wan yi*, one in a ten thousand).

However, there are not many words that can be turned upside down and still work effectively in English. Chinese is more flexible. Take footnote (*jiao zhu*), which can also be reversed to mean the same thing in *zhu jiao* (notefoot). Two instances come to mind straight away: *kai fang* (open) and *fang kai* (opened up) and *dong luan* (moving confusion, unrest) and *luan dong* (confused moving, dispersal). This second instance was a brilliant contribution to the Chinese lexicon from an *Otherland* contributor I knew and succinctly captures the contrast between the turbulent events in the lead up to the Tiananmen Massacre in 1989 and what followed: *dong luan* for social unrest and *luan dong* for people wildly and confusedly moving all over the place including overseas.

When I was teaching English in Wuhan, my students were

drilling in a conversation structure something like: "I have just bought a jet plane." "You are joking." Stuff like that. I was only subconsciously aware then but am fully aware now of the opposite ways in which we express the same idea about joking. That is, whereas the English say "You are joking", the Chinese have to either pose the question in "Are you joking?" or deny it by saying "Don't be joking!" For language instructors, this is a must-know aspect of the language or the languages.

In English we say, happy this, happy that, while in Chinese we say, this happy, that happy. For example, in English we say Happy Birthday, Happy Reading, Happy Go Lucky, etc, whereas in Chinese we say *kou fu* (Mouth Happy), *yan fu* (Eye Happy), *yan fu* (Sex Happy), etc. There's a bit of luck in all these Chinese expressions containing "happy" or *fu*. If you pay a surprise visit home and your family happens to have a big dinner, you may be described as being mouth happy. If you are in town and happen to witness a spectacle not normally seen you are eye happy. And if you happen to have a large following of women, you are then *yan fu bu qian* (sex happiness not shallow, a lot of sex happiness). Can you just turn them on their heads, Happy Mouth, Happy Eye or Happy Sex in English? Or perhaps you can, by just rendering them as happy eating, happy seeing and happy sexing, I suppose.

You might have noticed that when you say no you shake your head but when a Chinese says no he may nod his head. You know why? The English response to a question that requires the answer "no" is a "no" but the Chinese response to a question that requires the answer "no", for most Chinese who speak English, is a "yes", accompanied by a nod of the head. Thus if you say "I didn't like that film", your Chinese acquaintance might say "yes" to mean you are right that he didn't like the film. I notice that, even in greetings, Australians and Chinese behave in a reverse manner, the former shaking their heads from left to right while the latter nod.

It is important to note this difference above for in many court cases I have been through as an interpreter I know Chinese clients suffer because of their confusion in taking a no for a yes or a yes for a no. And I myself have taken offence at some Australians not nodding at me in greetings, wondering why these people are so rude!

Instead of directly referring to a woman as a prostitute or a whore, Chinese have a euphemism that describes their profession as "selling smiles". I had difficulty translating a reference to Sir Wong Hong Foo in William Lane's *White or Yellow? A Race War of A.D. 1908*, as being used to the "bought smiles and ravished kisses." "Selling smiles" in Chinese and "bought smiles" in English. So we sell and you buy or vice versa? What a nice pair of reversals!

So far, I have not mentioned a very basic and simple fact of reversal in regard to the order of our names. In English, surnames come second and given names first whereas in Chinese surnames come first and given names come second. Australians often call me Mr Yu instead of Mr Ouyang. Much of the bibliographical information compiled in this country still lists me under "Y". The Chinese are no better. After the general introduction in which Henry Someone and David Someone from the Australian side introduced themselves and their companies, the head of the Chinese delegation started calling them Mr Henry and Mr David! Somewhere in our heart of hearts, I suspect, there must be something turned upside down when we decide to live in each other's culture.

Similarly, Professor Wang added, the term "Mao's jacket", wrongly attributed to Mao, is commonly known in China as *zhong shan zhuang*, "(Sun) Yat-sien's jacket". Which makes me wonder if the Chinese do the same in translating other cultures into their own. In translating foreign names, they certainly do. Winston Churchill becomes Qiu Ji Er. Richard Nixon is Ni Ke Song. Charles de Gaulle is Dai Gao Le, their surnames becoming their full names and their first names all gone.

When the author of *Black on Black*, a travel book about her experience in Iran, mentions the fact that Farsi, the Iranian language is written from "right to left, so their books start where ours end, on the 'last' page", I am not surprised as that is exactly the same way in which Chinese was written for many thousand years (and still is in Hong Kong and Taiwan), until the 1950s when the Communist government in mainland China changed it to follow the Western way, a sign of irreparable Western impact or damage on Chinese culture. I mean can you imagine the English writing from right to left as a result of our influence? That has yet to happen even if it may take another 5000 years.

Filling out Australian forms often confuses the Chinese. They tick whereas they should only cross. Does the Australian form-maker know that the Chinese only cross when they say no and tick when they say yes? The only exception to this happens with the notice of public execution of someone in which a big red tick is put across the name of the person to be executed.

I am beginning to realise that if two languages, the Chinese and English, are so opposed to each other as to create so many opposites, the minds bred and born with either may be mutually opposed, too. I'll cite you one instance. A contemporary Chinese poet was recently very delighted with the publication of a collection of his poetry by a total stranger who did it without his permission and, indeed, without even his knowledge; he used this to show to his detractors how much he was loved and how good his poetry was. In Australia, by contrast, I did a similar thing by translating someone's poem because I loved it and posted it online for the Chinese audience to read, but this poet got so upset that she became abusive and wanted it removed at once. Now, you see how far removed these two different minds or mindsets are from each other.

This one I do not know where to place and have included here as a one-off as it perhaps confirms one stereotype that the Westerners have of the Chinese in their fictional representations (see my PhD thesis on this topic held at the Borchardt Library, La Trobe University), that of the vengeful Chinese. Lu Qiutian, Chinese Ambassador to the Netherlands, told a story of his experience working in the Chinese Embassy in Amsterdam. One day when he went to participate in an activity, the Dutch side asked which languages to choose for communications, English, German or French, as they felt sure that the Chinese did not speak Dutch. Deeply hurt by this arrogance, Lu spent a year learning Dutch and mastering it. When the time came again for another gathering, it was Lu's turn to pose a similar question, "What languages shall we use, Dutch, English or German, as I am sure you can't speak Chinese?". Perhaps, in contrast, there should be a reverse stereotype created of an ignorant but arrogant Westerner, I think.

A similar instance of reversal also occurred with Lu, mentioned above, when, on his delegation's departure, they exchanged gifts with their Dutch counterparts. The Dutch opened their gifts of silk immediately whereas the Chinese put their boxes of Dutch gifts in their own bags without even looking, making the Dutch wonder if the Chinese were not pleased. Similarly, one member of the Chinese delegation also wondered if the Dutch were not happy. If they were, why would they open the gifts to check in the Chinese presence, as if to see if there was anything wrong? Ah well, at least this much I can say for the Chinese: it is rude to look into a gift in the presence of gift-givers. The question is though, who should conform to whose custom in this sort of situation?

Many Chinese friends of mine, including university professors and authors, deeply resent the Australian coldness. They would tell you how they would welcome their Australian counterparts when they arrive in China by going to the airport to pick them up, taking them to their hotel and spending time to keep them company. They are astonished that this is not reciprocated on their arrival in Australia. They do have my sympathy here but then when I heard the Australian side of the story I grew to appreciate it, too. As an instructor of cultural communications for a big Australian company, I had the opportunity to hear the company director tell about his way of receiving Chinese counterparts: We expect them to organise everything themselves professionally and, instead of picking them up, we expect them to arrive at 9 am sharp the morning after their arrival. When the door opens at 9, they will see us all sitting around the table and waiting for them. That is our way of doing business. Without voicing it, I said to myself: And that is the sure way of scaring away your valued customers, mate, particularly if they are Chinese!

A well-known Chinese saying confirms this that goes, *xian zuo ren, hou zuo shi* (make person [friends] first, do things later) whereas the Australian way of conducting business seems to confirm that the reverse is true: do things first, make friends later.

Have you heard of the *guang ming de wei ba* (the bright tail)? If not, you are not aware of the Cultural Revolution and the 1980s China. No matter how bitter the tale is, its ending should always carry a positive message, referred to as the bright tail, a literary device employed in those times. Sometimes, this could be stretched to the opposite extreme as, according to Linda Jaivin, in an American film, titled *Johnny Got His Gun*, in which a wounded soldier declares that he wants to die. The Chinese subtitle changes this so it goes, "I must go on living!"

I received a shock when I read about the 100 Living Treasures in Australia in the newspaper; not that there's anything wrong with the phrase, but in Chinese "living treasures", or *huo bao*, means something entirely different. It means "a bit of a clown, a funny fellow or a lively person". I was relieved to see the Living Treasures turned into "National Treasures" in a Chinese newspaper the next day.

"All hell breaks loose" is rendered in a Chinese dictionary as "great confusion". Which is of course not half as good as when it is translated based on my theory of reversal. In Chinese, we have something that is similar in meaning but works in reverse, which goes *nao fan le tian* (heavens overturned or, more directly, all heavens break loose).

In English we say "God-fearing" but in Chinese we say, *jing shen pa gui* (god-respecting and devil-fearing).

Whereas Jesus is being tortured on the Cross, the Buddha is smiling. That is perhaps what makes the East and the West so fundamentally different, if only in appearance.

I met an editor of a literary magazine from another country, a Caucasian. We arranged to meet in Chinatown where I took him to have yum cha. The lunch, for the most part, was a happy one except for his insistence that I "should" take out a subscription to his magazine. Eventually I could no longer stand it and blurted out, "Look, I take you out for yum cha at my own expense" and you should have given me a free copy! I didn't say the second half of the sentence as it hovered around the tip of my tongue. The guy didn't seem contrite at all but said, "Well, I thought we are going to share the cost." In the end, I footed the bill for both of us and ended up with not a single free copy although he waved one from his bag at least three times just to show how good a job he had done in editing it and bringing it out. I am still resentful about it and perhaps he is too, about me not taking out a subscription. How are we, Chinese and Westerners, ever going to resolve our differences, our reversals?

4

Affair of the Heart

(Rick Springfield)

"Having an affair" is quite similar to the Chinese reference to having sex, "having a house affair", except that the latter refers to legal sex within the house between the husband and the wife.

I was translating Germaine Greer's *The Whole Woman* when I came across "two-timing" for the first time in a passage where the girl says, "Now I've made a mess of things by two-timing him with another lad." The translation having been published and got out of the way, I now want to point out we have something that means exactly the same in Chinese, *er xin* (two hearts), although I keep wondering what "time" has got to do with this and whether this *er xin* could come into use in my next novel or poem where I might say something like "two-hearting him" without raising any English eyebrows or English-speaking brows. As a matter of fact, I did eventually smuggle the word into my third book of poetry, now published, with the title of *Two Hearts, Two Tongues and Rain-coloured Eyes*.

I haven't read Eugene Nida's theory of equivalence in translation although I know he and his theory are revered in China. There is one thing I do know, though, which is that sometimes it just wouldn't do to match things up in two languages. I was watching *My Father, the Hero* on television with my son, who did not understand the word "sugar daddy"; nor did I, although I was quite amused by the no-sense it would make in Chinese. I checked the English dictionary, found its meaning and told my son what it meant but could not find its Chinese equivalent. The nearest thing to it was *xiao mi* (small honey), a reference to a young mistress. A nice pair!

In a conversation I had with my wife about male prostitutes in China, she referred to rich women who could afford to pay for their services as *fu po* (roughly, rich aunty). *Fu po* is a reference to rich women, often married ones, with a suggestion that they are not young any more even though they are not yet *po*, a granny. I was immediately struck by its similarity to the English "sugar daddy". Although it has no equivalent in Chinese these two could very well make a matching pair.

And, of course, there is a Chinese equivalent to the English sugar daddy that I only became aware of in late February 2003, which is *hua die die*, pronounced "deeye deeye", (flower daddy).

My eyes lit up when I saw this line, "love undrinkable as water", by Stephen Oliver for no other reason than that we have a common expression in Chinese used mostly by the cynics like my dead mother who used to say, "love uneatable as rice".

We are not that different, after all, even in emotions, which is how I felt when I came across "liquid embraces" in translating *The Shock of the New*, because the Chinese phrase that readily comes to mind is *rou qing si shui* (emotions as tender as water).

The "naturalist" tendency in Chinese language and literature is particularly strong in terms of love. If a woman casts amorous glances at a man, she is said to make *qiu bo* (autumn waves) with her eyes. If she falls in love with someone, she is said to *duo ru ai he* (falling into the river of love). If she is beautiful but marries an ugly or unmatched man, she is described as *xian hua cha dao le niu fen shang* (a fresh flower planted in the cow dung) as Chiang Kai-Shek's wife was once described. And if an ugly man wants to get the attention of a beautiful woman, he is said to be an "ugly toad wanting to eat the flesh of a swan". A woman's loving heart is normally referred to as *chun xin* (spring heart). A prostitute selling her body is described as *mai chun* (selling spring) and her client using her service is *mai chun* (buying spring). One euphemism for prostitutes is *feng chen nü zi* (wind and dust women). Even the Chinese word for "youth" is composed of two separate words, *qing chun* (green spring). When a man has a second marriage, he experiences a *di er chun* (second spring) and when he fucks around, he is *xun hua wen liu* (looking for flowers and willows). Do we have anything similar in English poetry? Robert Burns' "My love is a red red rose" is probably one of the few outdated examples that come to mind.

In Chinese, *hua* (flower) is an image for anything to do with pornography or affairs between men and women, as revealed in this activity that young men used to do in the past, *yin hua jiu, ting hua xi, bao hua niang* (drinking flower wine, seeing flower plays and embracing flower girls).

And, as a matter of fact, wherever a *hua* or flower is mentioned in the context, the English word sex or sexy can be substituted.

In another similar instance, a man, after having his first love affairs which he refers to as his first *tao hua yun* (peach flower fortune), describes himself as having a *hua hua xin* (flower flower heart) that would find it hard to resist any more temptations.

Prostitutes were given a range of nature related names in the old days, from *feng sheng fu ren* (wind and sound women), *ku hai ren* (bitter sea persons), *feng chen* (wind dust), *hua gu* (flower girls), *yan yue* (smoke moon) to *yan hua* (smoke flower).

And brothels, too, had "flowery" names in the past such as *feng yue chang* (wind and moon sites), *hua tai* (flower terraces), *hua hu tong* (flower lanes), *hua fen lou* (flower powder towers), *hua jie liu xiang* (flower streets and willow lanes) and *ji er xiang* (chick lanes).

And there is an old street in Wuhan, called *hua lou jie* (Flower Pagoda Street), that used to be a street lined with brothels before 1949.

I once saw a reference to Chinese prostitutes as *qian bo qing tiao*. Out of these four characters, three are words of measurement, respectively, "shallow, thin and light", the third word, together with *tiao*, meaning "frivolous and skittish". Except for the word "shallow", thin and light denoting a lack of seriousness are hardly translatable in English and form a weightless stereotype that forever dogs the working girls.

You say "fall in love with someone" but we say *ai shang le shui*, "love up with someone", not love down as the word "fall" suggests; perhaps I should translate it as "ascend in love with someone". Does that mean we as Chinese have more respect for the one we love than the English people? Or does it conversely mean that love is essentially a downward movement pulling one down towards one's love object or loved or loving object? Or perhaps it only suggests that while the Chinese stress the importance of respect in love their English-speaking counterparts stress the passionate headlong reckless precipitation?

There is an intriguing twist to the English "fall in love with someone" or, its Chinese version, "ascend in love with someone", in that when it comes to marriage, particularly a woman's marriage with a man below her in social status, the Chinese use the phrase *xia jia* (down marry or marry below someone), which a famous author uses in his essay when he mentions many beautiful Chinese women nowadays choose to *xia jia* themselves to the foreigners, meaning Westerners. In a way, Westerners ascend in love with Chinese women who end up marrying down with them. If you see how many young Chinese ladies choose to marry hoary-haired bleary-eyed Western men, you'll understand my point.

Wu Zetian (624–705), Empress Wu of Tang Dynasty, had a male concubine for her sexual pleasure, whose name was Feng Xiaobao, a wrestler and herbal medicine-seller, when she became the empress. This sort of "marrying down" or "mating down" strongly reminds me of Germaine Greer's recommendation that highly educated women should not confine themselves to men higher than them in position or learning but should enjoy the companionship of men their inferiors. Why not? Empress Wu set that brilliant example long ago by building a palace of male prostitutes for her own pleasure. She is roundly denounced, though, by Lin Yutang for her series of murders of her own family members, including her own brothers and sisters, and for setting up a spy system by which people were terrified into confessing what they did not do or say, and had to be beheaded.

We may say "heart dies" in English but we can't say "die-heart" as in "die-hard" whereas, in Chinese, "die-heart" (*si xin*) used as a verb is a most common expression. If you die-heart about someone, you no longer have any feeling for him or her.

We say "a bosom friend" while Chinese say "a know-heart friend".

We do both say "steal things" but *tou ren* (steal people), "stealing a man", is a specific reference to a woman having secret affairs with another man in her married life.

Furthermore, there is *tou qing* (steal emotions), a reference to having secret affairs.

The English word "skirt-chaser" has an even more imaginative Chinese counterpart, *bai dao zai shi liu qun xia* (prostrate oneself at the pomegranate skirt of a woman) or *ling chuan hong qun* (wearing another red skirt), meaning to have an affair with another woman.

Having an "affair" is too drab; you'd have "peach-coloured incident", the Chinese way to make it romantic. And of course the news related to that is "peach-coloured news".

Years back on a visit to Ottawa, I was told by a Canadian friend that there was not much "action" there at night. I remember my instinct immediately related this word "action" to sex. Interestingly, Chinese say the same thing. In a Hong Kong published book about the corruption of Chinese officials occupying high positions, one thing they often say after dinners at night is "find a place for action" (*zhao ge di fang huo dong huo dong*). But, of course, *huo dong* normally means "activity" and it's my translation that does the trick.

I have never thought of the Chinese word for husbands as anything special until I read a disillusioned Chinese wife's interpretation of it when she said that the husband is someone who is not a husband after a certain distance, measured by the Chinese *zhang*. The whole word is illuminated in that instant for *zhang fu* (husband) is a two-word combination that combines *zhang* (a Chinese measurement of length equal to 3.3 metres) and *fu* (man). Hence a man that measures three metres more in height (an exaggeration of course), echoing the Chinese expression *qi chi nan er* (a seven-feet man). In this case, however, this is a three-metre man who only maintains a three-metre relationship with his wife and will go for other women beyond that distance!

Years ago I read a lot of A. D. Hope and wrote an article about his concern with sex in his poetry. One image that frequently comes up is his reference to sexual experience with women as "reading them like an open book". Now, in *Lao can you ji*, a novel written by Liu E in 1904, the main protagonist describes his experience with prostitutes as *yue ren yi duo*. Meaning? Having read a lot of people!

I was reading *The Age* when the first sentence of an article about the tennis match between Michael Chang and Mark Philippoussis caught my eye. It is said that Michael Chang "wears his faith on his sleeve". Chinese expressions related to sleeves immediately come to mind: *xiu shou pang guan* (acting as an onlooker with one's hands in one's sleeves), standing by with folded arms, and *duan xiu* (cutting the sleeve), a euphemism for homosexual relationship, with a hidden story in it that tells of an ancient emperor sleeping together with his male lover. On waking, the emperor finds his lover lying across his long sleeve and, reluctant to wake him up, cuts it in half.

In a poetry reading held in mid-February 1999 in Melbourne, I heard a woman expressing in a poem her wish to have forty-two different friends coming to visit her on forty-two different days consecutively, followed by another set of forty-two friends. I was immediately reminded of a poem written by a Taiwanese gay poet, Chen Kehua, titled, "The fifty lovers living in my body".

When men are ejaculating, we say, "I'm coming". A Chinese man does that and says: *wo yao lai le* (I want to come). Eventually, they use the word *lai* (come) as a substitute for copulating like the word "cum", as in "I want to cum with you." Does that suggest that human beings, Western or non-Western, Chinese or non-Chinese, share the same feelings in having sex, even linguistically?

Just as you say cry wolf, so we say cry bed. We cry for different purposes. If we cry bed (*jiao chuang*), we make ecstatic noise in bed while making love.

A few years ago while I was attending a conference in Canberra on Asian connections, quite a city for that kind of thing, I learnt the use of the word "rooting" from a taxi-driver who told me how good a place Canberra was for rooting. I came across the same use of the word in a Chinese book about the recent rise of prostitution by female intellectuals in China, in which a prostitute calls the penis *nie gen* (evil root). The penis in Chinese is sometimes referred to as *chen gen* (the dusty root) as well.

In August this year I was talking to this fat security guy at Kangan Batman TAFE about a name for prostitutes in Hainan Island, which is *ding dong nü*, ding dong girls, because of the way in which they came to your hotel room and pressed the bell that gave a sound of dingdong. After a while, people would know straight away who was coming and for what purposes. This security guy said: "You know what dingdong means in Australian slang?" "What?" I said. "The dick," he said.

Gou yin, a Chinese phrase for "seducing", could be used for prostitutes who seduce their clients with sex but that is not the interesting part of it. The interesting part is that the word *gou* not only sounds exactly the same as the Chinese character "hook" but is actually the part that forms the character "hook".

Right now, I am enjoying a CD titled *Hot Brazilian Jazz*, while reading a book on Chinese women's one night stands or *yi ye qing* (one night love). I have just been reminded again how expressive Chinese legs can be. For example, the first one-night-standing woman in this book asks her third man whether he and other women *you yi tui* (have a leg). I must admit I like "have a leg with" much better than "have sex with" someone.

Years ago I translated a poem titled "Sleeping with woman" from the *Norton Anthology of English Poetry*, but it is only now that I have realised how the word *shui* differs from the English "sleep" in being a transitive verb. Instead of saying someone has slept with her, you just say, "he has slept her".

She says: I miss you! But, actually, this is my translation of what a character in my fiction says. In Chinese, that simply is: *wo xiang ni* (I think you)! Anyway, I was just reminded of a more colloquial way of saying it in Chinese in my local dialect: *wo qian ni* (I lack you)!

I often wonder about the creation of a word and what lies behind its intention or lack of it. Pubic and public, for example, are so close and so apart that you wonder why the twelfth letter, "L", is used to separate them, but its Chinese counterpart defies understanding. What is the connection of *chi gu* (shameful bone) to pubic unless it is implied that it is a bone most closely related to sex? Pubic hair, too, carries a note of shame in it when translated into Chinese as *yin mao* (yin hair) as if it were something inherently hidden and secretive, thus shameful when exposed, even though a man's pubic hair is also *yin mao*, not *yang mao* (yang hair), unlike his sexual organ, *yang ju* (yang tool), to which there is no female counterpart, e.g., a *yin ju* (yin tool), as a woman's sexual organ is, rightly perhaps, called *yin dao* (yin tunnel).

There are many euphemisms in Chinese for a man's penis. A common one is "little brother" (*di di*, pronounced *dee dee*); online, it is even shortened as DD. Another one is "second head". A third is "that word" (*na hua*). Recently I came across one that refers to it as "the shameful area".

Sometimes, English words, when translated, can find quite amazing and matching Chinese words. Take "groupie", which in Chinese becomes *gu rou pi* (bone, flesh and skin), someone who will make herself available in her bones, flesh and skin!

"Eye candy": I heard this for the first time while watching an SBS program on *The Boy* featuring Germaine Greer appreciating the young boy body. The eye candy is not something I can think of an equivalent to in Chinese even though we have *yan shi* (eye shit), *yan yao* (eye medicine) and *yan chan* (eye hunger). Not satisfied, I went online to do a keyword search for *yan tang* (eye candy) and returned with two items that I'd never known before: *xiang yan tang* (elephant eye candy) and *hu yan tang* (tiger eye candy). However, I have realised belatedly today that *xi yan* (eye wash or to entertain one's eyes with something delightful), would make a nice pair with this.

One Chinese word that sounds and means nearly the same as the English word "sex" is *se* (colour or colours), which means more than just "sex" or "sexy" but denotes "lascivious" as in *se gui* (sex devil), a term reserved exclusively for lascivious men, or *se qing* (sex sentiments or pornography). Although the Chinese don't have the equivalent to the English combination "sex cat", they have something similar, *se lang* (sex wolf), someone who is licentious, always a man.

My reading of a recent book suggests that the English "sex cat" has become accepted in the Chinese language, too; it is called *xing gan xiao mao* (small sexy cat or sexy kitten).

Cats in English are feminine just as foxes in Chinese are female. Now, with China more Westernised, not only the catwalk is widely accepted, called *mao bu* (cat steps), but even the cat or the kitten is accepted for women. For example, in Sichuan, the slang for prostitutes is *mao* (cats) instead of the commonly used *ji* (chickens or chicks).

I often wonder about the strong presence of Chinese women characters depicted as foxes or fox spirits in ancient Chinese fiction and the lack of such images in Western literature in general until I saw a sign that said "More Foxy Blondes".

Some Chinese expressions have gone out of currency, only to come back again with a vengeance. "Second Mother" (*er mu qin*), for example, as a form of address has lost its currency so that when I first came across it in a book about law cases in China I was taken aback because it sounded so strange in my ears. The case surrounds a dispute about the properties left to the plaintiff by the Second Mother of the defendant, the Second Mother being the second wife of their natural father. In place of this, a new word-combination, "Second Tit" (*er nai*), has come into use in recent times. The practice, initiated by Hong Kong businessmen in China, has spread across the southern coastal provinces, giving currency to the word.

To check accuracy in business translation, a recent trend in Australia is to find another translator to do a back-translation, either from or into the source language. It wouldn't do, I suspect, for a literary translation. For example, the transliteration of "massage" is now widely known in the Chinese diaspora as a euphemism for sex and appears in Chinese as *ma sha ji,* "horse killing chicken". Imagine back-translating that!

Water, Thy Name is Woman

(William Shakespeare)

If woman's name is "frailty" in English, then it is "water" in Chinese. Water-related woman images are so prevalent in Chinese literature that I wrote a Chinese poem based entirely on the direct quotation of those water-related lines from the poems by the Chinese poets, mostly male and occasionally female, such as this stanza from a not very well-known contemporary Chinese poet: "Women are so good/they grow up in water/they love us from the water/and this water is formed by their tears."

I've done a fairly long poem called, "Women are Water", which consists of a collection of set phrases, quoted from poetry and prose by others, used to describe women. Curiously, all of them suggest water, including, of course, lines about women by famous poets. When the poem was published, I read some more Chinese books and encountered more references to women as water. In one story, Jia Pingwa the mainland novelist actually named his main female protagonist as *xiao shui* (Small Water).

Even Cao Xueqin, author of the famed *Dream of Red Chamber*, was once quoted as saying, *nü ren shi shui zuo de* (women are made of water).

To add to this is the traditionally pejorative image of beautiful women as *hong yan huo shui* (red features, disaster water), meaning that beautiful women are the root-cause of disasters.

I found one of the few instances that link water to women in English poetry, I mean poetry written in English, by the New Zealand-based black poet L.E. Scott, whose poem "Woman" has a few lines that regard woman that way: "Woman/I look at you/And my mind swallows/Your whole liquid frame/I come in you/Like water ..."

The difference is that in this poem both the male poet and the woman addressed are water, as shown in the last line that goes: "We did come from water."

Last night I was reading a short story by a woman writer that was published in one of the most avant-garde literary journals in China called, *da jia* or *OM* (old masters?). She says in the story, quite expectedly, women are "like trickling flowing water". How can we deconstruct this tradition if women writers themselves still continue the myth?

If you are a feminist, you'd be amazed by how much prejudice there is in Chinese proverbs that are still widely acceptable and quoted. One recent instance is found in Han Shaogong's book *Insinuations* (2002), where he quotes: *shi shang zui du fu ren xin* (the most poisonous in the world is a woman's heart).

Wei Hui, whose novel *Shanghai Baby* was banned in China in

2000, writes that "the winter in Shanghai is like a woman's *li jia,* wet and disgusting". *Li jia* or routine holiday is a euphemism for a woman's period. It has an unlikely Hong Kong counterpart in *da yi ma* (one's great maternal aunt). Whenever a Hong Kong woman says, "My great maternal aunt is coming", she means her period comes around. And the basic form of this period is called in Chinese *yue jing, yue* for monthly and *jing,* full of significance, and among other things, for sutra or scripture, as in *fu jing* (Buddhist sutra or scripture) or *sheng jing* (the Holy Bible) or *shi jing* (The Book of Songs). Thus, *yue jing* (menstruation) could easily be "monthly scripture" or "monthly bible".

Women are not only often associated with water but also with plants in Chinese. I found an example in English in *The Whole Woman* by Germaine Greer, which I have just finished translating. In that book, she talks about women using "Firm Believer Body Toning Treatment" to transform "the orange-peel effect into the peach-skin effect". In fact, botanic imagery has long been part and parcel of Chinese descriptive vocabulary for women. The second part of the long poem I wrote in Chinese ridiculing that tradition is just about that. For example, beautiful women are often described to be "fragrant grass beauty", with "flower features and moon looks" that extend and display "flowery branches". For this reason, I call them "the vegetables", and, for the same reason, I call them animals because they are said to have "water snake waists", "goose-egg faces", and make "swallow sounds and oriole voices".

When it comes to women, you'd be surprised how most descriptions would resort to natural plants. A series of examples follow: *yang liu yao* (poplar and willow waist), *gua zi lian* (melon seed face), *liu ye mei* (willow leaf brow), *xing he yan* (apricot seed eyes), *ying tao xiao kou* (a small cherry mouth), etc. Now that man-made, or woman-made, objects threaten to engulf natural things, could we start describing them with new coinages, such as a remote-control shaped face, I suggest?

You wouldn't believe how far the Chinese can go with their analogy of women as water. In one Chinese article published in an Australian-Chinese newspaper, there are seven water-related images of women: "a woman after your own heart is tea", "a woman who intoxicates your heart is liquor", "a woman who moves your heart is soup", "a woman who softens your heart is vinegar", "a woman who persuades your heart is medicine" (I believe that is in liquid form?), "a woman who makes a mess of your heart is *xiang shui*" (fragrant water or perfume), and "a woman who makes your heart feel good is coke". What a load of crap!

"A young woman as beautiful as water with a heart as still as water." You know who is most likely to write this? Chinese, of course, this one being from a book on high-level official corruption in China.

Well, I have to revise this after reading what Germaine Greer cited as poetic evidence of stereotypes in English poetry, including Sylvia Plath who wrote that she was "A melon strolling on two tendrils"; Thomas Lodge who wrote, "I think with doubtful view/Whether you be the rose or the rose be you"; and Edmund Spenser who wrote, "Her cheeks like apples which the sun hath rudded" etc., exactly what I ridiculed in my Chinese poem.

Sometimes you can find similarities in most unlikely places. Take the Chinese word *po fu*, the Chinese equivalent to the English "shrew", "vixen" and "termagant". However, I am not happy with anyone of those English words simply because the meaning and sound of the word *po* is not brought out. *Po* in Chinese means "to pour" and sounds very much like "pour", too. A *po fu*, then, is a "pour woman", shrew, vixen and termagant all rolled in one, but she is more; she is a woman who "pours" out her feelings, be they anger, sadness, jealousy, frustration except passion.

And this "pour woman" was given an added dimension last night when I told Kirpal and Berni about it. Berni thought I said "paw woman" and that to me is even better because it signifies a woman who not only pours but also paws while expressing herself.

Michael Jackson has an album titled *Bad* that is translated into Chinese as *bang* (*Wonderful*). As "bad" is becoming "good" in English, it also took a turn for the better in the late 1990s Chinese culture, attested by a popular saying that goes: *nan ren you qian jiu bian huai, nü ren bian huai jiu you qian* (if a man has money he becomes bad and if a woman becomes bad she has money). This prevalent sentiment is echoed in a short story in which it is said, *nan ren bu huai, nü ren bu ai/nü ren bu huai, nan ren bu ai* (if a man isn't bad, a woman doesn't love him and if a woman isn't bad, a man doesn't love her). How true, exactly the reason why the divorce rates are so high these days in China!

Attesting to this badness becoming good is the publication of large numbers of trash books bearing titles with a "bad" in them, such as the one by Anna Wang in Taiwan, titled, *xin huai nan ren de shi dai* (*The Age of the New Bad Men*).

The situation involving women loving bad men has got badder with this remark: *nan ren yue huai, nü ren yue ai* (the badder a man is, the more a woman loves him).

There is certainly a parallel to Chinese badness in the West, testified by another song sung by Korn, called "Make Me Bad", which could easily be translated as it is in Chinese without raising a brow these days.

A few days ago, while listening to a comedian talking on Laugh Radio, I heard him say, "When she's good, she's very good, but when she's bad, she's very popular." Now, that's what "bad" is all about these days.

There is also an Australian parallel to the Chinese fondness of badness, exemplified by Dorothy Porter, who titled one of her articles in no uncertain terms as "It's too hard to write good – I'd rather write bad", in which she says, "I wrote bad because writing good definitely did me no good."

6

Sustaining His Life: *wei ta ming*

(Ouyang Yu)

When teaching English to native Chinese students it has to be pointed out that certain English words are gender specific, such as the ship and the cat, which have to be called "she" but Chinese people have no such gender preference. They are both "it" in Chinese. However, if you pay close attention to Chinese language, there is also a tendency to describe certain things in a gender specific way. Not so long ago, I had a Beijing-based poet sending a bunch of poems to me with a covering letter about himself, in which he expressed his wish to have a read of "her", the magazine *Otherland* that I edit. Indeed, in Chinese, literature seems "feminine". For example, an author's first work is referred to as *chu nü zuo* (virgin work or maiden work). When describing a city, Chinese also use the word "she".

An extreme example of male centrism would be calling a woman Mr, particularly when she is a nationally well-known leader, scholar or professor, such as Mr Song Qingling, wife of the late Dr Sun Yat-sien, Mr Li Yinhe, wife of the late novelist Wang Xiaobo, and Mr Yang Jiang, wife of the late Qian Zhongshu. How about calling Germaine Greer Mr Germaine Greer or Hillary Clinton Mr Hillary Clinton? This might be critiqued in feminist terms as "male chauvinist" because a woman has to be judged by male standards when she reaches the top echelon but I find the equivalent in the West as well. The most typical and common example is when a woman marries a man she has to take on the man's surname. A Chinese woman never does that these days although they did it in the old days when in written language "he" was indiscriminately used to refer to both men and women. This changed only in modern times when the Western concepts of "he" for men, "she" for women and "it" for objects and animals were introduced.

Still, in sound, there is no difference between "he", "she" and "it", as everything is pronounced *ta* in Chinese, which makes court interpreting a hell of a job. Imagine a witness giving evidence about a scene of domestic violence with these words: I saw *ta* last night before I went to *ta*'s place and there *ta* and *ta* fought with *ta*. Even though I have a way of dealing with it by putting it "he or she", "his or her place" and "he or she fought with him or her", it remains one of the biggest headaches for me that few outside the Chinese language could understand, let alone appreciate.

"Domestic violence" is not a term found in ancient Chinese vocabulary, as you can see from this story. Once upon a time, there was a general who had a concubine. One day the concubine stole into his room when he was asleep and found that he had good brushes and paper. She picked up one and wrote, "A colourful phoenix has to follow a crow." Just at this juncture, the man woke up and saw it. "This crow will beat the phoenix." As he said this he slapped her on her face till she broke her neck.

In *xi you ji*, pronounced *hsi yu chi*, *The Record of A Journey to the West*, a sixteenth-century Chinese novel, there is the *jin gu zhou*, the Incantation of the Golden Hoop, that is used by the Monk to keep the Monkey King under control; the words for *jin gu* actually stand for "tightening hoop" for the head. So, nothing is better than this when I applied it in translating Germaine Greer's sentence "tightening the headlock on the 'housewife'". We do not have the headlock in Chinese but we do have the tightening hoop that is equally efficient.

My father, now dead, used to refer to the government, the Party, and the top leaders in the third person as "it" or *ta*, either it or he, often in a very cynical and critical way.

Gender and prejudice are built into the language. One typical example in English is the word "history", his story, not hers. How can we neutralise this? Impossible unless we create totally new words. This is true of Chinese language, too. Take *ying xiong*, the Chinese term for heroes. The word *xiong* means male. So even if a woman is a *ying xiong*, she is still a male hero, not a heroine, because the word *ying xiong* is built with a male in it.

Taiwanese, as a result of being more Westernised, now have coined a new character for female heroes in *ying zi*, *zi* being females.

I wonder why national heroes are all men, such as Ned Kelly in Australia and Yue Fei in China, with the exception, perhaps, of Joan of Arc in France.

The world of business is a tough battleground that draws in all the young men, leaving women to play the communications games: people whose voices you constantly hear when you pick up the receiver and whose faces you constantly see when you enter the door of an office, in Australia, not necessarily in China. Have you ever had a woman ambassador like the Chinese one to Australia, Ms Fu Ying?

The "Other" translates into Chinese as *ta zhe*. Now this *ta zhe* hardly makes any sense if translated into English because it literally means "he person". In Chinese, anything that denotes alienness and otherness can be described as *ta* in the male gender. Examples are *ta xiang* (he land) for alien land; *qi ta* (*qi* he, for *qi* defies translation) for others; *ta ren* (he person) for another person or other persons; *ta ri* (he day) for some other time or some day; *ta sha* (he kill) for homicide; and *ta ma de* (his mother's) for damn it or blast it. There are two interesting points to observe here, one that to soften the effect of direct abusive language the Chinese prefer to use "his mother's" instead of "fuck you", preferred by an English-speaking person, and the other that in all those instances *ta* or "he" is never interchangeable with "she", pronounced in Chinese as *ta*, too. That is, the Chinese never say, "she land", "she day", "she kill" and "her mother's". Do we have anything similar to that in English? The answer is probably yes: them and us.

It has never occurred to me that the Chinese translation of "vitamin" could be an example of gender discrimination until my eye was drawn to the word *ta* in the Chinese translation/transliteration *wei ta ming* when I came across it in a book quite by accident. It reads, "sustaining his life".

And the word "exclusive" is made more exclusive in Chinese because it translates into *pai ta* (excluding him), not her!

It may be of interest to observe how Western feminists react to the Chinese word of "altruism" which I encountered when I translated Germaine Greer's *The Whole Woman*. As soon as I turned the word into Chinese I realised something fundamentally wrong because *li ta zhu yi* for "altruism" in Chinese means, literally, "benefiting-him-ism" although the word "him" is used to refer to all, much like the word "man" for "mankind" and all the people including women. I could have easily translated it as "benefiting-her-ism" in Chinese but that wouldn't make sense and my editor may simply dismiss it as unacceptable. Which is why I allow *li ta zhu yi* or "benefiting-him-ism" to stay uncomfortably in my translation of Greer's work.

If it is hard to understand why a famed female personality is known as Mr Someone, it is even harder to understand why her given name could be used as a surname. Recently, I was reading a Taiwanese book of anecdotes about various well-known Chinese writers when I came across the name of a famous woman writer Xie Bingying. She is not only referred to as Mr Xie Bingying but is also described as Mr Bingying with utmost respect, with Xie her surname cut for respect.

When I got my first email from a stranger who had the same name as my brother's in Canada, I told him that I did a doctorate in literature and I'd like to have him as my brother. The stranger was happy to be my brother but called me "sister" because he thought that if I did literature I must naturally be a woman.

Germaine Greer refers to men as "leaky vessels", which is quite reminiscent of a Buddhist reference to women as "empty jugs" that a friend of mine told me years ago in China. Interestingly, on a web poetry site in China run by the *xia ban shen*, the Lower-downs Group, men are referred to as *ba bing* (the handle) and women, *lou dong* (the leaky holes).

There used to be a set of strict regulations imposed on women in feudal Chinese society. The three obediences and four virtues are just that: Obediences to the father before marriage, to the husband after marriage and to the son after the death of the husband, and the four virtues of having morality, proper speech, modest manner and diligent work. Now the whole thing is reversed to what Dr Hu Shi describes as "the New Three Obediences and Four Virtues". The three obediences occur where the husband has to follow the wife if she goes out, he has to obey if she issues the order and he has to ignore it if she says anything upsetting. And the four virtues require that the husband must patiently wait when the wife is making herself up, he must remember her birthday, he must bear with it when she beats him up and abuses him, and he must be willing to part with his money for her to spend. After reading this, does your image of Chinese women stay the same? Or does this once again confirm your stereotypical notion of them as Dragon Ladies?

I thought I heard Jean-Paul Sartre referred to as "Mr Beauvoir" when I watched a program on television about Simone de Beauvoir's affair with an American writer called Algren or was it Simone who was referred to as "Mr Beauvoir"? I wasn't very sure and in any case I couldn't go back to where that happened as the program kept moving ahead. However, I think, it works either way, French or Chinese.

As I said before, my greatest difficulty in a court situation as a Chinese interpreter is with the gender. You never know who a client refers to when he or she starts talking about *ta*, like, *ta* said that *ta* killed *ta* and *ta* then moved in with *ta*. I have thought that there isn't such a problem with the English language until I had to translate a passage in Germaine Greer's notes to her *The Female Eunuch* (p. 379, note 2 under "Girl"), where she keeps using "they" in a context that makes it difficult to determine the gender of the people she speaks about.

The title of this book has a rag in it but I would never have referred to it as a she had I not read a poem by a contemporary

Chinese poet who keeps referring to an old piece of rag as "she", like "she began to soften/she really softened/she used her own dark colours to cover up the dust on the/table", in my translation.

There used to be a saying that went in China, *nü ren wu cai bian shi de* (the virtue of a woman lies in the absence of her talent), which was poignantly echoed by Henny in *The Man Who Loved Children*, where she says, "Men are always good to fools and perfect idiots ... A man will run ten miles from a woman with sense."

The curious thing about the gender is people never say 她杀 (she kill) but always say 他杀 (he kill) to mean murder. Our language (Chinese) has to change to accommodate the change as the number of women murderers grows.

Do human feelings have a taste? I think they do. The Chinese describe their jealousy (*ji du*) as "sour", as sour as vinegar (*cu*), which is why a jealous person is often known as a "vinegar eater" (*chi cu*). Interestingly, the English taste of jealousy is also sour, e.g. "sour grapes", suggesting that sour is perhaps the universal taste of jealousy. Chinese feelings have gender as well. Again, let's take *ji du* (jealousy)[嫉], which is formed of two characters, each with a radical on its left side denoting female gender as if this were a feeling unique to the women folk. Nowadays this could be changed as there are so many jealous men but you can't even begin to replace the woman radical with the man ones as the software has yet to be invented!

There's something I can never work out and that is the double meaning of "la jalousie" as both jealousy and the blinds. Maybe the French or the English will never understand why the Chinese associate the feeling of jealousy with women by adding the woman radical to the two characters *ji du,* 嫉妒 ? And when you come to think of it, the first character *ji* contains half a character for diseases and the second, a character for the door pronounced *hu*, something close to the blinds. And, as a matter of fact, *hu* (door) with a woman radical on its left side does come close to the other meaning of the word jealousy as being on guard if we take the door to signify her *yin hu* (yin door or vagina).

Finally, I must include my discovery about the word "Other" today; it contains "her". I found this out as I was driving out of the city onto the Eastern Freeway past a huge signboard bearing the word.

Doors of Perception

(Aldous Huxley)

I know you would say there is a world of difference between the two cultures, two peoples and two languages. A Chinese would say that's a difference between the cloud and the mud (*pan ruo yun ni*).

For underwear, we say "innerwear" (*nei yi*). And if a bird sits in a tree, we say it sits "on" a tree. This often keeps me wondering about orientation or, if you like, occidentation, and if Western eyes, or those of English extraction, are born to see things differently from the Chinese ones.

Reciprocation is fine, the kind of if you scratch my back I'll scratch yours thing that perhaps makes sense in any culture. It sounds cheap, though, to a Chinese's ears. It's like if you give me a lolly I'll give you one, too, when I have one, that is. The Chinese reciprocation for a favour done can stretch from a drop of water to the water of a surging spring, something I remember hearing the Chinese students saying when they were granted permanent resident status in Australia in or around the mid-1990s, certainly something for the money-smart Australians to tap into. To not beat around the bush any longer, the Chinese expression is *di shui zhi en, yong quan xiang bao.* Meaning? If you give me a one-drop-of-water favour, I'll reciprocate you with a return of water of a surging spring. Not something you'd do in this capitalist age, hey?

Qun xiao, "crowded small" or "crowds of petty people", is a term by which some high-minded ancient Chinese poets describe the small-minded people who constantly scheme, plot, talk behind backs and play all sorts of dirty tricks to advance themselves in their own best interest. But I like the description mainly because of the picture it gives of these people frozen in two characters, *qun xiao* (crowded small). I can actually see them now.

I had difficulty turning the expression "he thinks he is too good for us" into Chinese when it was used by a client at an interpreting session because if I translated as it is it would mean exactly the opposite, something like "he thinks he is better than us". On third thoughts, I went the other way around by turning it as "he thinks we are too bad for him".

Instead of saying a beautiful woman has a hard life, we say *hong yan ming bo* (red features, thin life). Meaning? A woman with beautiful (red) features has a hard (thin) life, as if life could be measured by its thickness. However, we don't say someone rich has a thick life; it doesn't work backwards. I remember Nick Jose telling us about hearing someone on the street calling life "paper thin". I suspect that, subconsciously, this Chinese thinness was at work, too, when Nick put that "paper thin" life in a novel. I wonder if it is a woman he wrote about.

How would you describe someone who is frivolous? Flippant? Superficial? Light-minded perhaps? Even light? Well, in this instance, the English language could learn from its Chinese counterpart as the latter has a two-word combination that measures the quality of frivolity with *qing bo* (light and thin).

We say *kan bing* (see sickness) whereas you say "see a doctor" about a sickness. In a sense, we cut all the crap, including the doctor.

Even when you introduce yourself to someone, you do exactly the opposite in two languages. In Chinese you say, "I'm so and so", but in English you just say "so", eliminating "I'm", cutting the crap in your own way. But this sometimes gives me a fleeting impression that the other party is calling me Susan or David.

Again, in reading an old novel, I picked up lost threads in simple words that I would normally overlook in reading contemporary fiction, such as *zhen zhuo*. Both characters with a left-side radical that denotes wine or alcohol, *zhen* means pouring it and *zhuo*, drinking it. When pouring the alcohol and drinking it, *zhen* and *zhuo* or *zhen zhuo*, it becomes the Chinese version of consideration or deliberation. I guess the ancient Chinese way of drinking may have been a slow and long process of sipping, involving much pouring and drinking in small cups. If you drink beer, the process will certainly not be one of deliberation but simply consumption.

I was stuck when I had to translate "for every ounce of fresh thinking, this overload produced a ton of incantatory jargon" in *The Shock of the New* for the simple reason that "thinking" is not measured in terms of volume in Chinese but by its depth or the degree to which it is "cooked". Hence *shen si shu lü* (deep thinking, cooked consideration).

About the use of "deep" to describe one's thoughts or ways of thinking, there probably will be no disagreement between users of English and Chinese languages. However, can we agree on using "cooked" along with "deep"? I see you are wavering, unable to make a decision but that's what Chinese have been saying and doing all along, thinking in a deep and cooked way, *shen si shu lü* (in deep and cooked thoughts), as mentioned above.

Bu jin qing li (not near feeling and reason) is a Chinese expression that is similar to the English "without reason" except for one important word, *qing* (feeling), because Chinese don't just reason with pure reason; they reason with "feeling", too. In fact, feeling and reason are one and the same, captured in the combination of *qingli* (feelingreason), causing no amount of confusion in Australian court cases involving Chinese clients as their tendency to temper reason with feeling often confuses the judges and the barristers alike.

You say "heartland" but we say *xin di* (heartland or heartground), two different things, though, for *xin di* can also mean one's moral character. And then the Chinese *xin* is such a word-combination generator that there are *xin fang* (hearthouse), *xin hai* (heartsea) and *xin lang* (heartwave), to mention only a few, once again proving incorrect Kirpal's theory that the English language is more expressive than the Chinese as there are things that can be expressed in the former that cannot be expressed in the latter.

The Chinese people have always thought with their hearts, not their minds, but it's only when the word combination suggested itself to me that I realised this simple fact, coded in *xin si* (heart thought). Then I remembered a common good wish, expressed in these four characters, *xin xiang shi cheng* (I wish you got whatever your heart thinks of).

The Chinese character *si* (thought) consists of two radicals (思), the field over the heart. In English, if you think of something, you have it on your mind, and, here in Chinese, it almost seems that when you have something on your heart, the Chinese equivalent to the English mind, it is the field that you think of, a concept that perhaps reveals the roots of the nation in agriculture going back many thousand years. The expression *xin tian* (heart or heart-field) further shows this link; an easy example is immediately found online where someone says that the seed of peace is sowed in the children's *xin tian*.

I was translating a commercial document the other day when I found it hard to turn one of the words into Chinese unless I twisted it around, vertically, so to speak. The sentence goes, "We are broadening our fundamental understanding" of something. Now to broaden one's understanding of something is virtually impossible because the Chinese people only deepen (*jia shen*) their understanding, not broaden. It's like you can have a broad smile in English but only a shallow smile (*qian xiao*) in Chinese. Well, I managed, as I said, to turn it from horizontally to vertically. Downwards, that is.

In the same way you measure one's smile by its width (broad smile), we measure one's tolerance also by its width, *kuan rong* (broad tolerance).

Although we don't say "a broad smile" we do say "a broad heart", as in *fang kuan xin*, have a broad heart or rest reassured.

My Australian PhD supervisor once accompanied the phrase "send up" with an upward hand movement, palm inward. That English gesture has no equivalent in Chinese, I am afraid, and would not make any sense in a similar situation. A Chinese expression that can probably match this is *yi zhi qi shi* (tilting the chin and showing airs), which describes a man of great power and high position ordering people around by slightly moving his chin forward and upwards without speaking a word, letting his airs do the work. Conversely, if I used my expression by tilting my chin forward, my supervisor would be baffled.

One gesture my wife says she never gets used to in her workplace is when her foreman holds up her forefinger with all the other fingers closed together, palm inward, flush with the nose, and bends her index finger inward, slowly, several times, to motion her to come over, without a word. She says that she feels very insulted by that because, in Chinese, if you want someone to come over to you all you need to do is raise your hand, palm outward, fingers pointed downwards, thumb pointed sidewise, and wave.

Xia bu wei li, meaning "not to be repeated for a second time", is a Chinese warning to the first-time committer of small crime like theft or shop lifting, which doesn't work here in Australia. If you are caught shoplifting, you'll have to go to court. Simple as that. However, there is a difference between the two systems with regard to capital punishment. Chinese, no matter how long they reside in Australia, cannot get past the idea that a murderer can go on living after killing more than one person such as the Port Arthur Massacre guy whose name I don't even recall at this very moment of writing. In China, if you kill someone, you have to pay for his or her life with your own life. Simple as that. I don't know which country is more democratic.

Despite all their differences, English and Chinese do have things in common from time to time. They have the same sense of directions as shown by these pairs: *shang xia* (up and down or from top to bottom), *gao di* (high and low), *yuan jin* (far and near) and *you wu* (have and have not). However, the Chinese language seems to have more pairs than its English counterparts, such as *da xiao* (big and small), *mei chou* (beautiful and ugly), and *qing zhong* (light and heavy). And these Chinese pairs form nouns that denote their closeness rather than their separateness, *shang xia* or up-down for height, *yuan jin* or far-near for distance, *da xiao* (big-small) for size, *qing zhong* (light-heavy) for weight, *pang shou* (fat-thin) for the size of a person and *chang duan* (long-short) for length, etc. Having found this out for myself, I am tempted to invent my own in English: life-death for a sense of human migration and poetry-prose for a new genre, such as the one I am writing here.

8

Spontaneous Combustion

(Webzine)

While many Australians may think themselves spontaneous as compared with Chinese who learn by rote and follow their leader like a herd, they are probably not aware of the spontaneity whereby the Chinese seldom or never plan their future but live on a day to day basis. In July 2004 when I was back in China again, I always booked my air tickets on the spur of the moment, like my fellow ex-countrymen.

I've just had an interpreting session with a Chinese delegation in a business promotion this afternoon. The Australian organiser gave a serious piece of advice at the end of it and wanted me to pass it on to the head of the Chinese delegation. He stressed the importance of beginning the preparation six months in advance, not two weeks as they had done. I had to point out to him that up to this very moment none of the Chinese delegates, including the vice mayor, had the habit of keeping a diary and that keeping a diary to record events to happen was a completely foreign and Western notion, exactly the opposite to the Chinese way of keeping a daily record (*ri ji*) of events that have happened. This was readily confirmed by one of the senior Chinese delegates who said, "We don't have to do that. If we want something to be done, it will be done right away. No need to pre-record it."

Whatever words we use to express the meaning of self-aggrandisement, we share one word in "blow" or "blowing". In English we say "blow one's own trumpet" or "trumpet blowing" whereas in Chinese we say *zi cui zi lei* (self blowing self beating) as in "beating a drum" or, more bluntly, *cui niu pi* (blowing cow hide). What has the act of "blowing" got to do with one's pride? Is that because one puffs out his chest when he feels proud and the act of "puffing" is similar to that of "blowing" itself?

When I read "If you can't dazzle them with brilliance, baffle them with bullshit" in Nick Jose's *Black Sheep*, something that happened a long time ago suddenly came back to my memory. In 1984 or thereabouts when I did a session with a group of Chinese and American engineers in Wuhan, one Chinese engineer was puzzled by what the American speaker said until the American guy said to me, off stage, "If you can't convince him, confuse him."

While the English say "pre-emptive", the Chinese say *hou fa zhi ren* (post-emptive). That is, they do not take action until someone else takes it first. I was reading a biography of Jin Yong, one of the most widely read contemporary Chinese writers of *kungfu* fiction, when I came across a remark he made about the difference between the Western military by making a "pre-emptive" strike and that of the Chinese as practised in *taichi* by taking "post-emptive" strike which, in most cases, is more successful than the former. I was amazed by the absence of the latter word, "post-emptive", in the third edition of *The Macquarie Dictionary*, suggesting a lack of the concept rather than anything else.

With this in mind, one can imagine the amount of resentment Asians had towards Australia when John Howard once mentioned Australia's intention to take pre-emptive action should it deem it necessary. From a Chinese point of view, this is totally unacceptable as the culture traditionally favours the post-emptive, waiting for the enemy to take the first step and lose the moral high ground.

In an article in *The Age*, a scientist is described as having the sort of "gung-ho shoot-first-ask-questions-later dedication", which immediately reminds me of the similar Chinese idiom, *xian zhan hou zou* (execute the criminal first and report it to the emperor later).

On 12 November 1999 I went to a poetry conference in Changping, Beijing, along with a lot of "postmodern" or "oral" poets. An outburst erupted when the young poet/critic Shen Haobo jumped to the rostrum and shouted his abusive language in the typical Chinese words, *ta ma de* (his mother's), to the angry amazement of some poet-listeners who reacted by saying this was uncivilised behaviour. Long after the meeting people were still talking about this in disgust. I was reminded of the launch of Arthur Boyd's exhibition in which Barry Humphries ended his launch speech with a tribute paid to Boyd by saying he was the "greatest bastard". I am sure this would be considered "uncivilised behaviour" by the Chinese poets when their language does not seem to allow the existence of anger.

Having written the above, I reconsider my position and find that the Chinese, particularly the young ones, do praise people with abusive language. *Niu b* (cow cunt or cow pussy, my own coinage), for example, used to be part of a phrase, *chui niu b* (blowing the cow cunt or cow pussy or cow hide or blowing one's horn, depending on how you pronounce it, meaning boasting), is now possibly the best compliment anyone can pay you if they think you are a good writer. The aforementioned Shen Haobo used this term *niu b* a couple of times to describe my poetry, *b xilie* (*Cunt Sequence*), recently published in *First Lines*, a New-York-based Chinese-language literary journal. A poet from Tianjin did the same. On the contrary, if the Chinese don't like a poet or his poems, they will say, "He is a *sha b*" (stupid cunt) or "his poetry is *sha b*". One recent written example is found in a book review by Yu Jian who praises the book as *niu b* and, on the side, criticises the age for having *sha b* getting the upper hand.

Many years ago, my father observed that English swear words are God related whereas Chinese ones are father or mother related. I think that is pretty much spot on, except that the Chinese swear words are more mother than father related. When the English say "For God's sake" or "God forbid", the Chinese might say "His mother's" or "Fuck your mother's cunt". Or, in male terms, the Chinese devalue someone's offspring such as sons and grandsons. *lao zi*, for example, is a general term for one's father. If I address myself as *lao zi* in talking to someone else, he or she will be offended because it implies that I am his or her father, but if I call him or her *biao zi yang de* (brought up by a whore) or *gou niang yang de* (brought up by a female dog, equivalent to son of a bitch), the reaction would be outrageous. In Beijing dialect, calling someone *sun zi* (grandson) is an even worse appellation.

9

Moral Fragrance

(Liu Yuxi)

Human excrement used to be removed by night which is probably why it was called "night soil" in English, but the weird thing is that although it was also removed at night in China it used to be called *ye xiang* (night fragrance) in Cantonese. Hence the expression, *dao ye xiang* (emptying the night fragrance). In this, you may detect the innate Chinese tendency to window-dress, door-dress and even word-dress so that it doesn't sound bad or ugly. Or else why is America *mei guo* (beautiful country), England *ying guo* (heroic country) and Germany *de guo* (moral country) even though we know America is often less than beautiful, England has nothing to do with being heroic and Germany, likewise, is not necessarily moral?

I was telling my son what "window-dressing" meant when I suddenly remembered that in Chinese we don't say "window-dressing" but we say *zhuang men mian* (door-dressing) which means the same.

Another example of reversal is one in which what is concrete in English is abstract in Chinese. For instance, whereas all the English poets, including Shakespeare, Shelley, Robert Graves et al, have associated scent or fragrance with flowers, the Chinese have done more; they have two words that no English words can match: *shu xiang* (book fragrance) and *de xin* (moral fragrance), I myself having come from a so-called *shu xiang zhi jia* (a family of book fragrance) and known a person with the name of *de xin* (moral fragrance), not to mention the fact that I know some lines by heart from that famous essay, "Epigraph on a Humble Hut" by Liu Yuxi, one of which goes, *si shi lou shi, wei wu de xin* (although I live in a humble hut I possess moral fragrance).

The English expression, "a match made in heaven", would be *tian zao di she* (made in heaven and arranged on the earth) in Chinese. It would seem that only in Chinese could anything half-made in English be complete. By implication, might I say that only when an English educated Chinese resorts to writing Chinese can he or she regain his or her integrity?

Chinese is such a balanced language. If you say "a thousand cuts", that sounds unfinished in Chinese unless you say *qian dao wan gua* (a thousand cuts and ten thousand slits).

When women in English beat their "breasts" to express their sorrow, Chinese beat their breasts and stamp their feet. Only in so doing their expression of sorrow is complete. There are many instances where for one complete English sentence two are needed in Chinese so that English sentences sometimes appear half-finished in Chinese. For example, in *The Whole Woman* there is a sentence that goes, "If we can find ways of harvesting the energy in women's oceanic grief we shall move mountains." The only thing I could do to make it read like a complete sentence in Chinese is to add the other half, whether it is intended by the author or not. I turned it into something like "We shall move mountains and fill the oceans", simply because we in Chinese say *yi shan tian hai*.

Try guessing the meaning of this: neither three nor four (*bu san bu si*). You might say that's "neither here nor there" or "neither one thing nor the other" but you are not right. "Neither three nor four" in Chinese specifically refers to someone of a shady and dubious character. A writer friend of mine living in Australia with limited English once gave it a more inventive twist by calling it "no three no four". Next time you see someone emerge from a brothel or a gambling den, you might describe him as a "no three no four" or a no-three-no-four good-for-nothing.

When we describe someone as "putting on airs", we are talking about his arrogant manners but manners is hardly a word to describe the Chinese word *qi* (air or airs) for there are so many Chinese characters, expressions and phrases that have "air" in them, each an impassable barrier for meaningful translation into English. For example, when someone gets angry, he is said to be *sheng qi* (generating air) or having *huo qi* (fire air or a fiery temper). When he is miserly, he is *xiao qi* (small air) and the opposite is *da qi* (big air). When he looks outlandish in a good sense, he is *yang qi* (ocean air), and if he is a bit of a country bumpkin, he is *tu qi* (earth air). When someone writes well with inspiration, he has got *ling qi* (soul air). Recently, a new word has come into currency, called *ren qi* (person air or people air), which is not found in any dictionaries yet but from its use in the newspapers I guess it means something like busy human activity with much human participation. In addition, "air" can mean trends and influences, such as *zheng qi* (square air or uprightness) and *xie qi* (evil air). That age-long practice of *qi gong* (air kung, kung as in kungfu) is a Chinese invention based on the idea of putting airs in good order within the human body for good health and longevity.

Actually, I think I've found a better translation for *qi gong*. As there is footjob, toejob, handjob, fistjob, tonguejob, even headjob, all sexually related, there should also be airjob, mainly emotionally or spiritually related.

I remember once remarking that poetry was an air that circulated within and without us poets that was invisible and unavailable to non-poets. An Australian poet in the audience agreed.

One thing I have found the hardest to translate into English without losing its original flavour, even meaning, is the character-combinations with the *qi* (air) in them, such as *gu qi* (bone air – strength of character or moral integrity), *xiao qi* (small air – miserly), *di sheng xia qi* (low voice and under air – humble), *pi li pi qi* (vulgar air – ruffian) and *liu li liu qi* (flow air – rascally). In any case, whatever you do to them in translation, you will never be able to keep the *qi* or air there, a case of inevitable loss in translation.

The other day I happened to be at the Victorian Writers Centre between two interpreting jobs. As it was quite warm, I made a comment on the unbearable heat, which elicited a remark from Chris. She basically agreed but added that she had found a solution to deal with the heat, namely, by mentally making a decision that it was after all not so hot and then relaxing. That is exactly what a Chinese expression, *xin jing zi ran liang* (when the heart keeps still, things naturally cool down), is about. I have a better translation for that which goes "a still heart keeps things cool" but my point in telling this anecdote is that sometimes one finds hard to describe a certain state of things in one's own language which can be easily described in another language because the expression for it has long been in existence. You don't have to mentally make a decision. You just use the old "still heart" expression.

The longer I live in Australia, the less I am homesick. However, when I was reading *Six Accounts of a Floating Life* by Shen Fu, I became so homesick that I wished I was back in China in my hometown to spend a summer, just for "the sound of the cicadas scraping the ears", as described in the book.

Shen Fu's wife, Chen Yun, said to her husband in *Six Accounts of a Floating Life* that she would like to build a house in a place that she liked, where he "will do paintings and she will do embroidery just for the sake of buying poetry books and rice wine. They can spend a life together content with cloth garments, vegetables and rice. And one doesn't need to plan for a journey far away". How I wish for such a life sometimes myself!

There is a Chinese idiom, *sui yu er an*, "to be able to feel at home wherever one is". I suspect that comes from Bai Juyi's line, "If my body and heart can find peace here, it will be my land" (*shen xin an chu shi wu tu*), echoed by Eastern Slope Su's similar line, "if my heart finds peace here, it will be my home village" (*ci xin an chu shi wu xiang*). This is quite similar also to Alex Miller's words, "to be in exile is to be at home, to be displaced is to be in place", except that the latter says it in a more English way.

Talking about this "word-dressing", it reminds me further that there is a lot in a name, particularly in a country's name. The worth of China dropped from that of china to anything bad that is associated with China or has a "China" in it the minute China got bashed by Great Britain in the first Opium War (1839–1842).

Hence China syndrome, Chinese burn, Chinese Wall, Chinaman, the last a pejorative term for the Chinese and an oceanographical term for a poisonous fish, indeed, hardly anything good. From that a conclusion can be drawn that, a nation, once bashed, always carries a bad name. On the contrary, the leading nations of the eight, actually eleven powers, that raped Peking in 1900 still carry grand names in Chinese to this day, as pointed out above in another context: *mei guo* for America: a beautiful country; *ying guo* for UK: a nation of heroes; *fa guo* for France: a law-abiding country; and *de guo* for Germany: a state of morality. To reverse this tradition, I think I did something in my book, *Songs of the Last Chinese Poet*, with Germans having germs, British being brutish and Hobart being Whorebutt. And can I also suggest an alternative name for America? *mei guo*, "mei" for mouldy. Hence a mouldy country.

I respect my wife's request to remain anonymous and so will always refer to her as "she" despite the critics' carping that I write about women without even bothering mentioning their names. The other day, she came back from work and told me that her boss would like to advertise for a new job vacancy. She first checked with her whether she had a friend or two to recommend but withdrew her remark by saying that it was a difficult position because recommended friends had been known to not work out eventually. True, I said, knowing from my own experience that things that began well did not end well in that regard. Then I recalled the Shakespearian title, *All's Well that Ends Well*, and commented on its closeness to the Chinese, *shan shi shan zhong* (begin well and end well). My wife disagreed. On third thoughts, I agree with her disagreement because whereas Shakespeare made a statement with that "ends well" remark, the Chinese expression is rather an imperative for things to both begin and end well.

10

Using the Pen Like a Tongue

(Zhu Ziqing)

Years ago I had a short friendly argument with Nick Jose when I was an MA student. I stressed the importance of literary appreciation (*xin shang*) whereas he talked about literary criticism. Then he said something, from my memory, to this effect: I don't see any difference between these two. But that's exactly where we differ. For we Chinese read a literary work the way we do a painting, not the way a surgeon does a piece of the human body or the way an invading army does a city by blasting it apart.

Nalan Xingde, a Chinese poet of Mongolian origins, is highly praised by the Qing critic Wang Guowei as writing a kind of poetry that is *xian chen bu ran* (not stained with an iota of dust).

What a nice way to write criticism!

I thought abhorrence of criticism a habit with Chinese writers until I met this Australian writer who told me that he didn't want to hear what nasty stuff the review that I came across said about his work. "Life is too short for such things," he said, which often sets me wondering but, of course, Chinese have an old saying that goes, "Men of letters belittle each other" (*wen ren xiang qing*). So, we are not so different, after all.

Sometimes you can find a perfect match between the two languages in question. Take "subtext". In Chinese, we say, *yan xia zhi yi* (what is meant under the words).

Years ago I met an Australian academic originally from America who referred to bad writing as "wet". Although we don't use the word "wet" we do describe bad writing as *shui fen duo* (containing much water). In Chinese, poor writing is described as "water injected books", derived, I believe, from the term *zhu shui rou* (meat injected with water so as to make the weight appear more than it actually is). In contrast, we refer to a piece of good solid writing as *gan huo* (dry stuff).

Some contemporary novelists write like a long, regular McDonalds. Every two or three years, there must be a novel, produced with machine-like precision. I do agree with Helen Demidenko or Darville when she said that she didn't have to do it that way and that if she didn't feel like writing she might stop it any time.

When I told an editor from Authors' Publishing House in China about *The Hand that Signed the Paper* and the scandal around it, to find out if it was interesting enough for him to consider the possibility of publishing its Chinese version, he said, "Who in China will be interested in reading something about Ukranians in the Second World War, written by an Australian?"

Fiction in Chinese is *xiao shuo*, "small talk". I have made a futile attempt to trace the origins of the word, for *xiao shuo* is not even found in *ci hai* (*Ocean of Words*), a Chinese dictionary that contains words and their origins. Ancient Chinese writers did not so much write as talk to their audience. They used their tongues, rather than their pens.

The recent emphasis on the orality in Chinese poetry may have simply stemmed from a desire to write like talking, as pointed out a long time ago by the essayist Zhu Ziqing, who said, *yong bi ru she* (using the pen like a tongue), and a remark made by Dr Hu Shi, *wo shou xie wo kou* (my hand writes my mouth).

I have forgotten the date on which Alex rang and revealed that the old Nordic word "saga" actually means "say", which I said was surprisingly similar to the Chinese term for fiction, *xiao shuo*, small say or talk.

Tom Griffiths in an article discusses "write up", a form of academic writing, versus "write down", a literary and creative activity. In Chinese, however, we say "write out" and, sometimes, "write down", but never "write up" unless a teacher asks a student to write something up on a blackboard. But "write out" is closely related to the Chinese word "write" or *xie*, which, as I have discussed elsewhere, rhymes with "giving vent to", "relieving", even "discharging". Hence the expression of something hidden within that bursts out, so prevalent in Chinese writings throughout centuries.

I arranged an interview with Rodney Hall in Shanghai when he was writer-in-residence at East China Normal University. He talked about the multiple meanings of the title of his novel, *Just Relations*. It is not till now that I am reminded many ancient Chinese books have titles of multiple meanings without meaning to be ostentatiously and fashionably modern or postmodern. Take *Sayings of the World in a New Language*. It could be interpreted in many other ways: *The World Speaks a New Language, The World Taking Delight in a New Language, New Stories and Tales of the Times* (Harvard university professor of Chinese Stephen Owen's translation) or simply, *shi shuo xin yu*. Same with *wen xin diao long*, a famous book of literary criticism, translated variously as *A Literary Heart Carving a Dragon, Carving the Dragon in the Heart of Literature, The Dragon Carved in a Literary Heart*, so on and so forth. The most interesting thing about the multiplicity of meanings in the Chinese titles, and this not found in many English novels, is the titles of novels formed by the part of given names of the main characters which in themselves carry meanings. For example, *The Golden Lotus* is originally titled in Chinese as *jin ping mei*, Jin for "gold" or "golden" forming part of the name of the first concubine, Pan Jinlian (Jin Lian is "golden lotus"), Ping (bottle or vase) is part of the name of another concubine, Li Ping'er (Ping'er is "a bottle"), and Mei for "winter plum" is part of the name of the third concubine. Thus the whole thing actually means *Gold Bottle Winter Plum* or possibly *A Winter Plum Blossom in the Golden Bottle*. You can't have more meanings than this.

The Chinese term for "the reader" is *du zhe*, the character *du* rhyming exactly the same as "lonely", which is an apt description without meaning it. Hence *du zhe* for a reader and a lonely person.

In English and Chinese, we now refer to readers as readers. But in classical Chinese literature, readers are respectfully referred to as *kan guan*, literally, looking officers or reading officers. I don't know how that came about but I am reminded of the position of a reader at a university nowadays in, say, Australia. Isn't that a kind of reading officer?

Yi Sha had a line that he seemed to like very much, which he also used in an unpublished novel he sent to me for consideration for publication in *Otherland*. The line, from his poem "The Hotel", goes, "When I woke up/my cigarette/was beautifully burning/in her hand." If there are two meanings one can read into ancient Chinese poetry, the surface and the political, there are equally two to read into the post-1990 Chinese poetry, the surface and the sexual.

Reading *The Biography of Xu Wenchang* by Yuan Zongdao, I am again deeply moved. I read it a couple of times in China many many years ago and I read it in Australia for the first time six years after I left China. I had an entirely different feeling this time. By comparison with Xu the poet, Van Gogh the painter is small wine, not beer. Yuan writes, "As Xu got older, his anger deepened and he even shammed insanity. When the important people came to his door, he refused to let them in ... Sometimes he hacked at his own head with an axe, covering his face with blood and breaking his skull with a noise. At other times, he pierced his ears with an awl, inches deep, but, surprisingly, did not die. Zhou Wang said, 'His poetry and writings became even more wonderful in his old age but nothing was published and everything was hidden away in his own home.' ... Wenchang lived a life unfulfilled and died in anger." [English translation mine]. I don't know if I shall live a life similar to his in Australia but I do share his contempt for the mediocrity of the writings of his contemporaries and his status of being a free spirit rejected by the powerful and the rich. Technically, the small size of this biography is extremely appealing, beating any contemporary Western biographies that I hate to read; it is only five paragraphs long.

At one of the numerous book or magazine launches in Melbourne, Gig Ryan and I were introduced to each other. The very first thing she asked me was, "Why are you so angry in your poetry?" I said, "I thought you were the one who was angry and it was for this reason that I used to translate some of your poems that I like, such as 'If I had a gun'." There are at least two Chinese phrases that come to mind: *fen nu chu shi ren* (a poet is born out of anger) and *hen ren*, meaning a poet is a "hate person".

In reading poetry, I often get it wrong, not because I do so deliberately but because my eye slips, so to speak, seeing a wrong word for a right one. For example, in a poem where it is said, "I confessed to him my anthrophobia", I thought I saw "I confessed to him my authorphobia" and I actually thought mine better.

I love mispronunciations if only because they give me creative edges not easily available in the correct and polished ones. The other day I heard someone speaking of "perfection" as if it was "perfiction" and I said to myself: God, aren't novelists these days perfictionists. Just look at the obsessive ways in which they write and revise. I'd rather be a poet, doing it at one take, like fucking.

Eastern Slope Su or Su Shi, the famed man of letters in Northern Song Dynasty, talked about writing as *xing yun liu shui* (drifting clouds and flowing waters). The English or English-speaking writers, who tend to revise, revise and revise, seem to prefer a quality of limpidness as suggested by the "limpid English prose" (Robert McCrum *et al.*), suggesting to me a quiet stagnation which I often find in their literary works.

Chinese have a saying that goes, "An article does not tire of being revised for a hundred times." That being right, a person does get tired of revising an article for a hundred times, particularly a poet.

Who's reading poetry these days? Not a market researcher. Nor an airplane pilot. Nor a prime minister. Nor a minister. Nor god himself. Nor a nuclear scientist. Nor a pawnbroker. Nor a confectioners' supplier. Nor a roof plumber. Nor an airport taxi controller. Nor an accident assessor. Nor a wholesaler. Nor a rubbish collector. Nor a dentist. Nor a cool room builder. Nor a computer room cleaner. Nor an underwriter and undertaker. Nor a theatregoer and telemarketer as well as a telephonist. Nor a tour guide. Nor a tennis coach and a long-distance coach driver. Nor a second-hand dealer. Nor a seedsman. Nor a sign-writer. Nor a wall finisher. Certainly not a poultry (pronounced poetry) farmer.

Having said that, it is time to revise it after a number of security guards in the Wuhan building housing the School of Foreign Languages and Literatures in which I worked temporarily as a professor have asked for free copies of my Chinese collection of poetry, *xiandu* (*The Limit*) because they liked it.

As I am printing this final draft, I am visited by an old episode in the Australian-Chinese cultural exchange. In the late 1990s, I remember, I was invited to a one-day seminar held at the Australia Council, where I witnessed an intense conflict between a Chinese professor and an Australian translator over whether translation should be funded in favour of dead authors over the living ones. Although the Australian seemed to have won the battle, the words, said by the Chinese professor, still ring true in my ears: "If a dead author's work is of great value, it should be translated. Likewise, if a living author writes rubbish, the fact that he is still alive doesn't warrant translation."

Huang Yuanshen, professor of Australian literature in China, included a single essay in the entire volume of *An Anthology of Australian Literature* (1997) on the basis of poor quality of Australian essays as a whole. By comparison, the essay is a very mature form of literature in China. It is in fact so mature and uniquely Chinese that some of the best essays defy translation into other languages.

After finishing reading Paul Hoover's *Postmodern American Poetry: A Norton Anthology* (1994), I felt dazed, impatient and weary; I skipped through the last part including the poets' essays as appendices. It is enough to say that the poets' ideas or theories are better than their poetry. I was strongly reminded of a theory recommended for all men and women of letters in the Great Proletarian Cultural Revolution (1966–76), which promoted that "themes or ideas ought to take precedence over everything else" and resulted in the death of vigorous and lively writing. The same thing seems to be happening here; even that abhorrent idea itself, promoted so widely during the Revolution, I suspect, might have also come from the West originally.

I hate to meet famous people. In a reading where famous Australian poets were surrounded by admirers I simply walked away. It's the same with Chinese writers. A guy told me excitedly that Wang Meng was giving a talk in town a few years ago and asked if I'd like to go. I thought about it for a minute and said, "No". My reason for this is simple: I feel tired of having to say nice things and to look up at someone when talking to him or her simply because of their fame. Admiring people who are no longer there or here and whose books I like is easier and more equal. Refer to my authorphobia, mentioned before.

11

Saving Face

(Alice Wu)

Face is one's identity. The closest English equivalent to Chinese in terms of face is "lose face" and "save face", which I suspect came from Chinese originally. However, there are more set phrases related to the face in the Chinese language, such as *ai mian zi* (loving face), loving one's face, being concerned about one's reputation; *zheng mian zi* (fighting face), fighting for one's face, winning honour or bringing credit to someone; *yao mian zi* (wanting face), wanting one's face, suggesting the desire to keep up one's appearance, and *si lian*, dead face. If someone is a "dead face", he or she is shameless. In English, a limited language, though, all speakers seem to know is "lose face" without knowing its other side, e.g., "want face", "love face" and "fight face".

A current expression in China that incorporates "face" or the *mian zi* is *mian zi gong cheng* (the face project), a project that is put on show for the sake of showing off without much relevance to the local needs or conditions. For example, according to a report on Chinese Yahoo, a poor county in China spent millions of dollars in building a so-called Century Square with huge sculpture and lawns but many of its small towns did not even have access to roads. The locals have come to call the square a "face square".

Culture still refuses to be translated despite the best intentions in the world and skills, too. Let me just cite one example. In a Chinese story about a corrupt public prosecutor, it is said that people vie to get his attention by trying to bribe him and they are described as "tearing their faces" to do that. Hence one more addition – "tear face" – to the growing number of new coinages based on the "face".

I often see this picture on television of Australian people involved in a court case being filmed. They sometimes cover up their own faces or alternatively hold out their palms to cover up the camera. It suddenly dawns on me that *they* also are afraid of losing *their* face. So, this fear of losing one's face is not unique to Chinese culture – despite what is said in so many cheap books written by Westerners.

If you can say "give someone the go-by", why can't you say "give him/her the face" (*gei ta yi ge mian zi*)? Meaning? Giving someone a chance not to lose his or her face, a widely used expression in China. Hence my coinage, "give face".

From "face value" I was able to coin my own phrase "face meaning". Whereas in English we say we can't take something at its face value, we say in Chinese that we can't just translate anything at its *zi mian yi si* (face word or, more exactly, word face), meaning that we can't just take the words as they appear at first sight.

In my hometown, people talk about sex in a very direct and brutal way. They say *zhu ri pi gu, ren ri lian* (a pig fucks the bums as a man fucks the face), meaning a pig fucks from behind whereas a man fucks because of the (beauty of the woman's) face. In Jia Pingwa's sex-infested novel, *fei du* (*The Capital in Ruins*), there's a similar but more subdued and censored saying, *nan ren x nü ren shi x lian de* (men x women mainly to x their faces), "x" being the Chinese sign of "fuck," similar to your "f—k".

It would be hard to relate Dunlop, the brand name for a tyre, to the cheek, but in the recently published Chinese dictionary of 12,000,000 Chinese characters on Chinese dialects, there is a reference to Dunlop or Deng Lu Pu in Chinese translation and transliteration, as meaning "cheeky", "having the cheek", or simply "having the thick face skin", taking its origins in the thickness of the tyres of this brand. Using this as an example about what I was going to write in my book, I was talking on the phone to Carolin Window, a novelist from Brisbane and AsiaLink writer in residence at Peking University. I mentioned how some Australian reviewers looked at my second book of poetry, *Songs of the Last Chinese Poet*, as "in your face" stuff, and that reviewers said the same about Mark Davis's *Gangland* – and that I'd always write "in your face" stuff as long as I am in Australia. Carolin suggested that I might link this with the reference to Deng Lu Pu.

One of the Christian tenets about tolerance is if someone strikes at the left side of your face, you should present the right side. I have thought that there is no such thing in Chinese culture until I came across the Chinese expression, *tuo mian zi gan* (spitting face self drying): when someone spits in your face you should just wait until it dries up by itself!

While they say "skin deep" as in "beauty is but skin deep", we say "skin shallow", as in *fu qian* (skin shallow or shallow). One Chinese writer once said, "Beautiful people are all skin shallow." As shallow as the skin, not deep enough.

The English expression "a broad smile", mentioned before, does not translate easily into Chinese as people of that nation don't measure smiles mathematically by the width or length but by the way the owner of the face opens it up or spurts out the rice he is eating or claps his hands or faces the sky or covers up his mouth.

The only food-related smile in Chinese that can remotely match the Australian "cheesy grin" is *pen fan* (spewing rice), which, however, means laughing so uncontrollably that one spews out the rice one is eating. I, no cheese-eater, still have to work out how you grin with cheese. Or do you mean you grin with all your teeth buried in cheese or your face smeared with cheese?

In a recent lecture on B.E. (broken or bad English), I coined my own abbreviation, LMBTO, based on the English LMAO (laughing my arse off), mine meaning: laughing my teeth off, based on the Chinese saying that goes: *xiao diao le da ya* (laughing my big teeth off).

Smiling from ear to ear is your way of smiling, as illogical as our way of smiling from the nostril (*bi zi yan li xiao le yi xia*).

The mouth is a dangerous organ in Chinese, as shown by these two expressions: *bing cong kou ru* (diseases come in through the mouth) and *huo cong kou chu* (disasters come out of the mouth). Further, there is a saying that goes, *san jian qi kou* (one should put three strips of seal across one's mouth to avoid saying something wrong). In the Tang Dynasty, Empress Wu had a wooden ball placed into a criminal's mouth to stop him saying angry things to upset her. In the Cultural Revolution, the communists were more extreme. They cut out the tongue of Zhang Zhixin, a woman communist, to stop her from telling the truth. Such things may not have happened recently in the West but the saying "speech is silver, silence is golden" hides a similar fear. The only difference, I suspect, is that Westerners are better self-censors with their mouths.

Reading a biography of Fu Lei, the celebrated Chinese translator of French literature, I was intrigued by the use of a Chinese expression, *pou fu jiao* (belly slit friendship), friendship to the degree in which you slit open your bellies to show each other the hearts, which reminds me of something similar about the kind of friendship *ge tou huan jin* (cutting off the heads and exchanging the necks), for the kind of friends who will do anything for each other. I doubt if this sort of friendship still exists in contemporary China.

12

Let's Get Physical

(Steve Kipner/Terry Shaddick)

A barrister I interpreted for in the County Court said something to his client to this effect, that he could not predict what the judge's final word would be because he could not get into his mind. When I translated it, I put it as "get into his heart" because Chinese think with their heart, not mind, testified by the common expression *xin xiang* (heart thinking). This reminds me of what D.H. Lawrence's Connie did in *Lady Chatterley's Lover* by feeling things "in her womb" and what one of Alex Miller's characters did in his novel *The Ancestor Game* by feeling in his "gut". Do we, Chinese and English, think or feel with so vastly different organs?

"We think with different organs," I began. "While you think with your mind, we do with our belly." "But that's not entirely right," Bruce said. "Because we say gut feeling." "Yes, you are right," I agreed. "You say gut feeling and we might say gut thought or gut understanding. How's that for a swap?"

The belly is a treasure house of knowledge for Chinese people. When the Chinese say *xin zhi du ming* (the heart knows and the belly understands), they simply mean they "know it". If someone is described as *man fu jing lun*, he is having a bellyful of "statesmanship" or "statecraft." It is interesting to observe that the belly in English is not a place for knowledge but for food as we all know from such words as "belly worship"; to that we might add "belly calculation", which is exactly what a client does in Leslie Zhao's fiction when he is trying to work out which of the faces of the prostitutes are nicer.

Can you turn "fruit" into a verb? You can, but only in Chinese. We say *guo fu* (fruit the belly), originally meaning to fill one's belly with wild fruit but now simply meaning to quench one's hunger.

Genet sounds blasphemous when he says, "The idea of God is something I harbour in my bowels", but it's really yet another instance of gut feeling. With the word "idea", it even carries the suggestion of Chinese gut understanding or gut idea.

A Chinese person must laugh differently from an English-speaking person. As the latter "splits his or her sides" with laughter, the former only "holds his or her belly with laughter" (*peng fu da xiao*). I guess they probably laugh the same way but their languages condition them to laugh with different organs.

During the 1998–1999 summer holiday, to prevent my son from wasting too much time, I borrowed a copy of *Oliver Twist* from the library for him, which he enjoyed reading. Sometimes he would tell me what he had read or asked questions about certain words he didn't understand, such as "quartered" when someone was threatening that Oliver would be "drawn and quartered" if he did not behave. I had to explain this in Chinese but suddenly found I could not because the Chinese way of saying it was very different from the English. Instead of cutting someone into four pieces by "quarter", we cut him into eight big pieces by *da xie ba kuai.*

Sometimes amazing links can be found between English and Chinese in both meaning and sound. Take the English surname "Lynch". I was watching a television program one night in which someone by that name was being interviewed and, all of a sudden, the Chinese word *ling chi* came to mind. And they are such a hair-raising pair! Now you all know what "lynch" means but the Chinese *ling chi* is even more horrific in that it is an ancient way of punishing the prisoners by dissecting his limbs, similar to the English word, "quartering."

Is fear generated in different organs depending on our nationalities and races? My suspicion is that it is or else why do we say in English "the lily-livered man" whereas we in Chinese say "the small-galled man"? Or is the Chinese gall equivalent to the English liver?

I have yet to find anything interesting about the English organ "liver" apart from "liverish". The Chinese *gan* (liver) serves more positive purposes. *Xin gan bao bei* (the heart and liver baby) is a lover who is after one's own heart; *gan dan xiang zhao* (the liver and the gall shining upon each other) describes the utter devotion shown to a friend; and *gan nao tu di* (the liver and the brains smearing the ground) again shows a kind of devotion in which one is willing to die the cruellest death for one's friends or superiors even if it means he has to spill out his liver and brains!

You might wonder what one's chest has got to do with knowledge or skills but I received a Chinese-language magazine from America yesterday in which a short story I wrote in Chinese appears. While flipping through the pages, I was pleased to see an old expression like an old acquaintance, *da fu gao* (drawing up a belly draft), which is the Chinese way of making a mental draft of an article, similar to the expression *xin suan* (heart calculations or doing mental arithmetic), the Chinese way of making a mental calculation, similar again to the expression, *cheng zu zai xiong* (with bamboos in one's chest), containing the gist of the story of an ancient Chinese painter who did paintings of bamboo well because he had "bamboos in his chest", chest being the Chinese storage of artistic skills and knowledge, of course. Hence the Chinese ways of writing an article in the belly, doing the sums in the heart and painting in the chest.

The Chinese belly is also a receptacle of tolerance, shown in an old expression that goes, *jiang jun e shang neng pao ma, zai xiang du li neng cheng chuan* (a general has such a vast forehead that a horse can run on it and a prime minister has such a big belly that you can row a boat in it).

An excellent piece of literary writing in Chinese could be described as *dang qi hui chang* (literally, sweeping airs and turning around in the bowels, and, approximately, splendid or majestic). Now how could that have anything to do with one's bowels? But that's the way the Chinese describe their good writings all along, as if this kind of writing had a function of opening one's bowels at the time of constipation, and I suppose it is similar to the way they refer to drinking to one's heart's content as *kai huai chang yin* (opening one's bosom to drink profusely).

We in Wuhan do have something that is so vulgar in relation to one's arse that it hardly bears repeating. Nevertheless, I shall put it down here for my I-wouldn't-care-less Australians. The expression for the miserly people goes: *kou pi yan, suo zhi jia* (which roughly translates as "You are so miserly that you scratch your arsehole and then suck your finger").

By the way, *pi yan* (arsehole) in Chinese is not even the arsehole but the arse eye or the eye of the arse.

Fear is often associated with shit or excrement perhaps because it has the potential to induce it from us whether we are Western or Chinese. We say "shit-scared" in English and *xia de pi gun niao liu* in Chinese (so scared that fart is rolling and urine is running).

I had thought there is no equivalent in English to Chinese "fart" in meaning until we had our Italian friend Frank, who's married to a Chinese woman, over for dinner. When I taught him how to say "nonsense" in Chinese by saying *fang pi* ("That's a fart" or 'That's nonsense") and explained what it meant, he said, "We have a milder form, 'hot air'."

Just as "shit" is easy to find in contemporary Australian poems, "fart" abounds in Chinese poetry and prose, perhaps because the Chinese fart is frequently used in daily language to mean "nonsense". I was recently surprised to come across poems containing fart references by some unknown men of the past. One of these is a monk who wrote a volume of poems titled *niu shan si shi pi* (*Forty Farts of Cow Mountain*) and the other is Shi Chengjin who also wrote a volume of poems titled, *fang pi shi* (*Farting Poems*). I wish I could lay my hands on these farting poems but the writer who referred to them did not give any clues as to which historical period these guys belonged to. Anyway, I am comforted by the fact that Chinese are as down-to-earth as any Westerners and make no pretensions to being aristocrats who don't fart.

I was first attracted in China to Patrick White by the surprising number of farts his characters make in his short fiction. Then I noticed that the English fart is not really an "f" with "art" in it because it does not generate many varied expressions. For "I don't give a fart about that idea", we have something very similar in Chinese, *guan wo pi shi* (it's none of my farting business). But for *you hua jiu shuo, you pi jiu fang* (If you have something to say, say it, and if you have something to fart, fart it), it would be hard to make a connection. That is because in Chinese we say "What a fart!" instead of "What a nonsense!" or "What crap!" One classic example of fart being introduced to poetry is when Mao Zedong says in a poem, released not long before his death, words to the effect that "It is not necessary to fart!"

I often wonder what a fart sounds like in English although I know how it does in Chinese. It sounds exactly like *bu*, as Yi Sha makes amply clear in one of his poems. In Chinese *bu* means "no". However, if I ever get a situation where I have to find something to match the sound of a fart in English, I might resort to the word "boo" because it sounds so much like the Chinese *bu*.

When it comes to one's arsehole, the Chinese are most reticent. They don't even favour it as an abusive weapon like they do in English: "You are an arsehole!" I did come across a reference recently in one of Wang Xiaobo's essays, in which he uses a colloquialism, possibly current in Beijing but not in Hubei where I come from, that goes: "You are one of those with an arsehole so big that your heart drops out of it", meaning you are very careless. Now you know what that reminds me of? Not even remotely related to it but I still would like to tell you. In my first visit to Canada, I was so amazed and attracted by the sumptuous variety of foods available that I always ordered more than I could eat at each meal. So the head of the Canadian organisation said this to me, "Ouyang, you have eyes bigger than your stomach." That was in 1986 and I never forgot it.

The English "balls" for men's testicles is surprisingly similar to the Chinese character *qiu* because it sounds exactly like the

Chinese word for ball and has a radical on its left side indicating hair, in the picture of a tuft of hair surrounding a ball：毬 .

Viagra, the virile medicine, has acquired an interesting Chinese name in Australia, *wei ge* (great brother) and I am amused to see it turned in yet another version, *wei er gang* (mighty and steely).

Do we have any use for the intestines? The Chinese have at least two kinds of feelings in relation to them: sadness and regret, as seen in such usages as *chou chang bai jie* (sad intestines tied into hundreds of knots) or *duan chang ren* (man with broken intestines) and *hui duan le chang zi* (regret it so much that one's intestines break). It could almost be said that, in replacement of the English "heart-broken", a new coinage could be adopted, "intestine-broken", based on the aforementioned expression.

"Stretching the intestines with a hanging belly" (*qian chang gua du*) describes a deep anxiety or worry about things a Chinese, often a Chinese woman, feels. Again, the Chinese feel anxious in their bowels rather than in their hearts.

You say "a sweet tooth". In contrast, we say "a sweet mouth" (*zui tian*), a mouth of honeyed words. Which brings us to the Chinese expression *kou mi fu jian* (mouth honey and belly sword): someone who says nice words but hides daggers in his or her heart or, literally, his or her belly, an unseen aspect of the belly that is revealed here: a place where you hide harmful hatred as well.

"Palpitate"? Is that how you describe a heartbeat? Well, in sound maybe but not in the image. I'll show you something: 忐忑不安 (*tan te bu an*), a Chinese expression about how one does not feel at ease. Each of the first two characters has a heart radical underneath but the radical over the first heart means up and that over the second heart means down. Hence the picture in which a heart beats up and down uneasily, indicated by the sound of it, too, *tan te* (pronounced as *tan ter*). Try saying it a couple of times to yourself.

"Gut-wrenching passion". You wonder if that is a borrowing from Chinese for in Chinese there is an idiom that goes, *gan chang cun duan* (the liver and the intestine broken by the inches).

One language's brains is another one's intestines. Why? *Sou suo ku chang*, the Chinese expression that literally means searching through one's dry intestines, is usually given the dictionary meaning of racking one's brains for fresh ideas or apt expressions.

In temper or spleen, both Chinese and English agree that it is the organ with which they vent their spleen or *fa pi qi* (have spleen air or tantrums). Whereas in English spleen is always bad, in Chinese it can also be good, e.g., a good-spleened person.

Do we have any use for the "gallbladder"? The answer must be in the negative because, I guess, anything related to "gall" must be as bitter as "gall and wormwood" or as malicious as in "a pen dipped in gall". However, in Chinese, the word, *dan* or "gall", meaning courage, has more than a dozen different uses. Lack of gall is lack of courage, so people who are timid and cowardly are described as *dan xiao gui* (small-galled devil) or *dan xiao ru shu* (as small-galled as a mouse). On the contrary, people who are bold are said to be *dan da*, have "big gall" or "a big gallbladder", sometimes so big-galled that they are *dan da bao tian* (have such a big gallbladder that it wraps up the sky), from which *se dan bao tian* is derived, meaning to have such a big sexual gallbladder that it wraps up the whole sky. In plain English, it means one will do anything driven by sexual desires.

There's one thing that links the English and Chinese nose, which is money. When I read about Stella McCartney making Madonna "pay through the nose" for a new dress, I was reminded of a remark my mother made years ago about me.

"People with tiny nostrils are known to be misers," she said, "because they are so small that coins don't drop through." When I was translating *The Man Who Loved Children*, I came across a similar reference where Jo, Sam's sister, said, "A big nose means a generous nature."

One more example of the Chinese nose-related expression: "hit a noseful of dust". Meaning? You fail to get anything you try to get and end up getting a noseful of dust.

In English, American and Australian literatures of days gone by, Chinese are often described as "slit-eyed" or "slanty-eyed" but few notice that the typical feature of a Westerner including anyone from those three countries is the "big nose". While there's a large borrowing of food-related Chinese words in English such as *dim sim*, *yum cha*, and *chow mein*, one word related to the "nose" is completely ignored, which is the slang, "beezer" (not available in the Macquarie Dictionary, the Third Edition) that closely matches the Chinese character for the "nose", pronounced *bi zi* or "bee zer". Having said that, I want to point out that in Chinese the number of set phrases related to the nose is few, about as many as that of the set phrases related to the brow in English. I don't know whether the nose, like the arse-hole, is disliked for its unpleasant emissions and again I don't care but I am interested in finding out about the difference that makes Chinese Chinese, English-speaking people English, and also the possibility that English can be made somewhat Chinese and vice versa. I can think of only two set phrases that are made out of the nose. One is *yang ren bi xi* (relying on the breath from someone else's nose), which describes the dependency of a person on the pleasure of others, certainly not a very pleasant status. The other one, *bi qing lian zhong*, again a very unpleasant one, means "with bruised nose and swollen face", obviously referring to someone in a bashed state, worse than "a bleeding nose". There are words and expressions that have the nose in them, too, *bi zu* (nose ancestor), one's earliest ancestor or originator of a tradition and school of thought, and *you bi you yan* (having nose and having eyes), used in a situation in which someone makes the story sound quite convincing. On the other hand, there are so many set phrases related to the nose in English that I am simply daunted by the effort of having to quote them all here except one, which is "a nose of wax"; the nearest Chinese equivalent to it is "a soft ear".

It is not as though we are very different, I mean Chinese and English or Australian. For example, we can simply turn "in the twinkling of an eye" into *zha yan jian* in Chinese without missing anything because it takes "the twinkling of an eye" to blink or wink, in both languages anyway.

You can't give the Chinese a "black eye", because it doesn't make linguistic sense although it does make physical sense as it would anywhere in the world. Equally, you can't give the English or Australians a "white eye" (*bai yan*), again for the same reason. In Chinese, to give someone a "white eye" means to look down on him. To do this, you would have to turn your eyes up or sideways until the whites are shown.

Well, I have to revise my view here for just now I came across a reference to Ruan Ji, the poet of Western Jin, who was well-known for giving people the "black eye" (*qing yan*) and the "white eye" (*bai yan*), depending on whether he liked you or not, the "black eye" showing his respect and appreciation and the "white eye", just the opposite.

My son remarked in the car on our way back this afternoon from Vietnam Street, the Chinese version of Victoria Street in Richmond, Melbourne, that Chinese musicians don't seem to favour jazz at all; he himself is a passionate lover of jazz because he plays both clarinet and saxophone. I agreed with him, saying that that was only because Chinese musicians considered themselves too highbrow for such lowbrow stuff as jazz, choosing to play classical instruments such as piano, violin and to sing Italian operas. Then I had difficulty explaining what highbrow means in Chinese with matching words because "highbrow" does not make sense if put into Chinese word for word.

I was amazed by the lack of set phrases associated with the word "brow" in English. Besides "highbrow", we only have "knit one's brows" and it only expresses the feeling of anger. In Chinese, by comparison, the brow is an expressive organ of happiness, calculation, confusion and many other aspects of human emotion, unmatched in English: *xi shang mei shao* (delight on the tip of one's brow); *mei tou yi zhou, ji shang xin lai* (when one knits his brows, a good idea comes to mind); *mei mao hu zi yi ba zhua* (trying to get brows and beard all at once), trying to solve problems indiscriminately without sorting them out properly; *mei fei se wu* (with dancing brows and radiant features – enraptured or exultant); *mei kai yan xiao* (brows open and eyes smiling – all smiles); *mei lai yan qu* (brows come and eyes go – making eyes at or flirting with each other); *mei qing mu xiu* (brows clear and eyes pretty – having delicate features); and *mei mu* (brows and eyes – prospect of a solution or sign of a positive outcome). This often makes me wonder about the limitations of the English language in relation to human organs and if the English speakers can detect anything more than just anger from a Chinese brow. Much would be lost in cross-cultural communications if one is not prepared to know something about brow-reading.

It is not until I came back to China recently to teach that I came to know or re-know an essential feature of Chinese culture, long lost to me. The key description of it would be *huoshao meimao* (fire-burning the brow), a situation in which one leaves everything to the last minute till one's brow is burning before one takes action to resolve it, to extinguish it, so to speak. I'll tell you the tale. The big sign over the School of Foreign Languages and Literature, Wuhan University, had somehow got wrongly put the Chinese way as Wuhan University Foreign Languages and Literature, a sharp contrast with the other sign in another building, just across the square, School of Law, Wuhan University. Even though professors and academics were keenly aware of this problem, no one did anything about it until an international conference was going to happen in a couple of days. The day before it happened, they began chasing people, including me, about the right way, and decided there and then to change the order. Since then, many things have attested to this brow-burning phenomenon as contrasted with the Australian way of planning or fixing things well ahead of time.

I don't know from which English organs anger issues, unless we stretch the meaning of "liverish", but when a Chinese describes his or her anger they are most likely to say that their "lungs burst open with anger" (*qi zha le fei*)

I revised my opinion when I realised that there are a number of English words related to the brow, such as "frown", "glower", "lour", "lowering" and "scowl", and that every word except "lour" has an "ow" in it, even the "ou" in "lour" similar to the "ow". I'm not an etymologist and never want to be one but I suspect this "ow", like the Chinese character *mei* 眉, written in the shape of an eyebrow over an eye, also reveals the original intention of the English word-maker to give shape to the word by putting the "o" of an eye next to the "w" of a brow even if their position is a little out of shape. But I have yet to find more functions for the English brow than just "frowning", "glowering" and "scowling", etc, etc, and even "browbeating".

When a Chinese knits his brows, he is not necessarily angry; he is probably deep in his thoughts. When an English-speaking person wants people to read his lips, a Chinese may understand it to be that he wants people to find out how his mouth moves. When an Australian raises his brows, he expresses surprise, but when a Chinese does that, he conveys a feeling of delight. Indeed, the Chinese expression *yang mei tu qi* (raising the brows and breathing out airs) actually means "to hold one's head high" or "to feel proud and elated."

In Chinese, "lips" or *chun* are not a very expressive linguistic organ. So far, we've got only five set phrases, all from the ancient times, and very few lipped expressions, so few that the Chinese "mouth" has to come in whenever there are English lips. For example, "button up one's lips" is translated into Chinese as "keeping one's mouth shut", "escape one's lips" as "escaping one's mouth", "pass somebody's lips" as "entering somebody's mouth", "seal somebody's lips" as "seal somebody's mouth", and "lip-service" as "mouth-service" (*kou hui er shi bu zhi,* favour shown by mouth but not done in deed). However, the Chinese lipped phrases are not to be missed for their literary imagery, e.g., *chun qiang she jian* (the spear of lips and the sword of a tongue, or lip spear, tongue sword, or, more Englishly, battle of wits or words) and *chun chi xiang yi* (the lips and the teeth clinging to each other, a mutually dependent close relationship) or *chun wang chi han* (when the lips are gone, the teeth will feel the cold), which are self-explanatory, as well as *chun hong chi bai* (red lips and white teeth), used to describe a handsome young man.

Teeth must be used for the same purposes of endurance in both Chinese and English cultures as shown by the English "clenching one's teeth" and the Chinese *yao jin ya guan* (tightly biting the tooth gate). However, both go to the extreme with their teeth. In English you sometimes clench your teeth whereas in Chinese you "break the tooth and swallow it" or "break the tooth and swallow it with blood", showing a steely will to withstand the pain.

This morning I was listening to someone complaining about the opening ceremony of the Sydney 2000 Olympic Games on Fox Radio in my car when I noticed that he used "long in the tooth" to complain about the length of a certain program. I forgot about the program but quickly scribbled the phrase onto a stick-on for I recalled the Chinese saying about something similar, which is *lao diao le ya* (so old that the tooth drops off). Actually, it could be fittingly translated as, "old in the tooth".

I deliberately pass lightly over eyes, ears, the face, the tongue, the mouth, the teeth, simply because there are so many phrases built around them in both languages that I would like to draw attention to other little things like the spit. You would think the English are a very cultured race until you know the phrase "spit in the eye" of someone – which certainly tells you what the English are capable of, both in words and in deeds, for I have seen that happen in Australia. None of the words associated with "spit" such as "drool" or "slaver" is suggestive of food except the expression "my mouth waters" but then in Chinese "spit" or "phlegm" is immediately linked with one's strong desire for food or something one treasures, such as *chan xian yu di* (desirous saliva is on the point of dripping), a line from one of Su Shi's poems written about 800 years ago. Or else, "saliva" or *tuo mo*, along with "snivel" or *bi ti*, can be found in such a phrase as *shi ren ti tuo* (picking up someone else's snivel and saliva), which means "plagiarising" or "copying other people's creative or original ideas". The longest-standing "saliva" phrase is perhaps *xiang ru yi mo* (keeping each other wet with one's saliva) from one of Zhuang Zi's fables thousands of years ago that tells how fish in a dried pond keep each other alive with their saliva, a tale of mutual help in adversity.

The first time I came across the reference to someone with a shifty eye was when I read Xavier Herbert's *Capricornia* with the half-Chinese character Ket. Then a policeman joked with me during an interpreting session by saying I had shifty eyes. I thought it would be hard to translate this into Chinese, as we don't use it that way, until I read a book on face reading. According to that book, if someone has eyes that float about and never stay in one place, he or she is said to have *zei yan* (thief eye) as against someone with stable eyes that indicate the possession of a stable character that won't harm others. In that instant, I realised that the so-called shifty eye is really what the Chinese call the *zei yan*.

"I am all ears", when translated into Chinese, becomes *xi er gong ting* (I wash my ears to listen with all respect). In a recent development, the Hong Kong Chinese has extended the "washing ear" image to mean "listen to music" and expanded the image to include "washing the stomach" (*xi wei*) to drink the drinks and "washing the eyes" (*xi yan*) to see the movies.

Once, my son's music teacher commented that he had a "very good ear". For the same reason, Chinese also refer to good musicality as having good ears. Nie Er, composer of the Chinese national anthem, had a nickname, *er duo xian sheng* (Mr Ears). Indeed, after he acquired that name, he changed his name to Nie Er, which in Chinese is four ears, as shown here: 聶耳, 耳 (pronounced *er*), being an ear.

Following from above, I said to my wife that translators often have to sacrifice a lot in order to make sense. For fear that a direct translation of "I am all ears" does not make sense to the Chinese readership, they will find something equivalent, which is the Chinese *xi er gong ting*, for the simple reason that there is no "all ears" in Chinese. I mean how many ears are "all ears"? Two ears or 100 ears? And what does "all" really mean?

Similarly, if we do the same thing by turning *xi er gong ting* into the English "I'm all ears", we lose the "washing ears" image. So, that is what this book is partly about. It's about what is lost in translation and what can be gained by it.

I thought of helping my younger brother out of his trouble with the Chinese authorities on my way to the County Court for a job the other day. Those Chinese words immediately came to mind: *zhu ta yi bi zhi li* (helping him with an arm's power or, literally, to give him an arm), meaning to give him a hand. Curiously, at the same time, the English "arm" visited me, too, with the phrase "keep at arm's length". It is obvious that Chinese and English use their arms for different, sometimes opposing purposes.

We lose different body parts. As an English-speaking Australian, I lose heart. I lose my mind. I may even lose myself. As a Chinese-speaking ex-Chinese, I lose foot (*shi zu*). I lose hand (*shi shou*). If I were a woman, I could lose body (*shi shen*). Need I explain at all? All these three losses in Chinese mean more than they look: "losing foot" for making an irreversible mistake; "losing hand", a euphemism for "losing one's mind" when one uses his hand to strike out at someone without thinking; and "losing body" often referring to a woman who has lost her virginity. In Chinese, however, we don't say "lose heart", even among seventy-nine expressions with a "lose" in it.

13

Yahoo is an Elegant Tiger: on language animals

(Ouyang Yu)

One thing about "Yahoo" on the internet. Its Chinese equivalent is pronounced exactly the same as *ya hu*, "an elegant tiger"!

One wonders why the Chinese describe the slapdash ways of doing things as *ma ma hu hu* (horse horse tiger tiger). My guess, as good as yours, is that when someone draws a tiger it resembles a horse but he doesn't care either way.

What is *hu ya* (tiger tooth)? you might ask. Easy. It is the third tooth leftwise and rightwise from the upper front teeth on either side and they are so called because they bulge and won't be concealed by a smile or any smile. You see this in many people, Chinese or foreign. For some reason, it did not find its way into a Chinese-English dictionary, perhaps because the lexicographers did not happen to have the tiger tooth or teeth themselves.

Chinese heroes are often depicted in positive animalistic images, I suppose, because of the availability of such terms as *hu bei xiong yao* (the back of a tiger and the waist of a bear). For example, the Party Secretary Li, in one of Chi Li's stories, is one with a "tiger's back and bear's waist". Personally, I strongly disapprove of such stereotypes.

The use of *lang yan* (wolf smoke) by a Chinese poet in a recent poem caused a temporary loss of my linguistic memory as I have not come across that for a long time. Not only can we not find a match for it in English but the expression also has run out of currency in the Chinese language. It is in fact the smoke from burning the wolves' dung in ancient China to signal impending danger at border posts. Still, I can't help but like it for what it is by the look of it and for its very remote connection to your "cry wolf". These days you can hardly find a wolf to cry about, least of all the wolf's dung to burn.

I remember reading an article about sex and the cat but pity is I can't find it when I badly need it to refer to for this stuff I am writing. Different from the English cats that generate so many expressions and phrases and things feline, female and sexy, the Chinese cats lack the power of expression although the cat is also an object of contempt as in *mao shu tong mian* (cats and mice are sleeping together), meaning the superiors and their subordinates are collaborating for wrongdoing, and also in *ah mao ah gou* (Ah Cats and Ah Dogs), a contemptuous reference to despicable people hanging together.

I read an interesting article in *The Weekend Australian* about cat-haters in the West, particularly their association of cats with women, as reflected by words like "kitten", "cat-walk", "pussy", "slinky", "queening", etc. It took me a long time to go through the 6,800 idioms in a Chinese dictionary, only to find a single idiom that is related to cats, which is the above-mentioned *mao shu tong mian*. The only other reference to cats is *mao ku lao shu*, "a cat weeps over a (dead) rat", shamming sympathy that one doesn't have. In any case, it is true that the Chinese do not associate cats with their women although "cat-walk" has been accepted as part of contemporary Chinese terminology solely reserved for fashion models. I was just finishing this near midnight when my wife came in, saying, "Well, I've now become a 'night cat' like you," which in Chinese means, "I'm a burner of midnight oil."

That very familial reference reminds me of a description my mother gave of my father, calling him a *hua jiao mao*, a flowery-footed cat, for his habit of not liking to stay indoors for long without going out.

The Chinese expression, *jiu si yi sheng* (nine deaths and one life), describes a narrow escape from death, as compared with the English, "a cat has nine lives". If an English cat has nine lives, he or she is capable of having "nine deaths one life" in the Chinese sense.

To "let the cat out of the bag" is something that the Chinese do not have but the expression, *mao ni* (cat greasy), a very recent one, so recent that it has not found its way into any dictionaries yet but is present in Chinese newspaper stories, online and on living lips, caught my attention today when I came across a news item in *Guangzhou Daily* which used it in the title without any explanation but made enough sense for me to understand that it meant something suspicious.

When I translated the word "lackey" which Marigold likens Ket to in *Capricornia*, I used the word "a dog's leg or running dog" (*gou tui zi*), not surprisingly, considering the general negative Chinese attitude towards dogs, which brings to mind a string of dog-related idioms in Chinese: *gou ji tiao qiang* (when a dog is hard pressed, he will jump the wall), a reference to bad guys who will resort to anything when cornered; *gou xue lin tou* (dog's blood spurts on one's head), terribly abusive; *gou zhang ren shi* (a dog relies on his master's power), lackeys acting as bullies because of their master's power; *gou yan kan ren di* (a dog's eyes look down on people), about a snob; *gou shi dui* (dog's shit heap), a most disgusting and hated person; *gou pi* (a dog's fart), absolute nonsense. Dogs are good for one thing in parts of China, though: eating. I have eaten dogs myself but that's another story.

It's funny to notice how the Chinese try to match their idioms with the English ones. For example, the Chinese equivalent for "love me, love my dog" is *ai wu ji wu* (love my house, love my crow [that perches on it]).

Charles Baudelaire once lamented the helplessness of the albatross teased and mimicked by the sailors, saying, "How awkward and feeble he is! Not long ago so fine, how grotesque and ugly!" While totally agreeing with him, I cannot but help remember the old Chinese saying that goes, "When a tiger drops on the plain, he is bullied by the dogs." Recently, I came across a pen-note story in *shi shuo xin yu* (*Sayings of the World in a New Language*), written in the fifth century, of how a princess so loved raising cranes that to ensure her crane would not fly away she cut his wings. "The crane looked at his cut wings and lowered his head, looking dejected. Lin then said, 'If he has this gesture of reaching the clouds, how can he bear to be raised for the pleasure of one's eyes and ears?' And she raised him until the wings grew again and set him free."

In *Capricornia* "This country's been settled donkey's years", wasn't difficult for me to translate but it reminded me of a similar Chinese expression, *hou nian ma yue* (monkeys' years and horses' months), only used as a negative statement, such as this, "I don't know what monkeys' years and horses' months this will take us to get there."

I am sure that a pig's liver doesn't mean anything in English although a pig's whisper does. In Chinese, we generally refer to someone flushed in the face as being flushed the colour of a pig's liver (*zhu gan se*), in the negative sense, mostly for men. Translating "Gigney flushed crimson" when mocked by the imp in *Capricornia*, I was indecisive about whether I should turn "flushed crimson" into "flushed the colour of a pig's liver" as the latter had strong negative connotations the former didn't have. In the end, I settled for the neutral "crimson".

When Xavier Herbert describes Mark, the "uninvited guest", coming home to Red Ochre "as sodden as one could be" in *Capricornia*, I had to resort to the Chinese expression, "as sodden as a chicken dropped in the soup" (*luo tang ji* or drop soup chicken), as it describes that kind of sodden state. For future use in English, I suggest, the expression could possibly be changed to "chicken soaked in the soup" or something like that.

Translating where Tocky in *Capricornia* "dashed about like a lantern-baffled possum", I resisted the temptation to turn it easily into an equivalent Chinese expression "like an ant on a hot wok" because the possum is native to Australia, not the wok.

Of Mice and Men, a novel by John Steinbeck and also a line from Robert Burns, was translated into Chinese as *ren shu zhi jian*, literally, "Between Mice and Men", thus losing its original significance. However, what I wanted to say with this is that for mice Chinese reserve no respect whatsoever. *lao shu guo jie, ren ren han da* is a well-known Chinese proverb that means, "When a mouse crosses the street, everybody cries to beat it up." Mice, like dogs, are not kindly treated in the Chinese language. Our mice-infected words are *wu ming shu bei* (one of anonymous mouse generation or mean creatures), *zhang tou shu mu* (with the head of a buck and the eyes of a rat: repulsively ugly and sly-looking), *shu mu cun guang* (the eyesight of a rat is only inch short: short-sighted), etc. Thus it is no wonder that Mickey Mouse, very popular with Chinese kids, is an American invention, translated into Chinese as *mi lao shu* (the Old Rice Mouse), creating one of few instances in which the mouse is given a positive image. And the other neutral image is, of course, the mouse that you use beside the computer, called *shu biao* (the mouse pointer).

Carp have an important place in Chinese literature and culture, which makes the Australian lack of respect for carp even more conspicuous. Carp are sold at A$2.00 a kilo in the fish market and, as I observed and later wrote into one of my long Chinese poems about the Murray fisherman, carp were stoned to death and thrown back into the Murray. I told the story to my Australian friend who was taking private lessons in Chinese from me when I taught him a Tang-dynasty Chinese poem partly about carp. The last two lines go, "There has been a peach-blossom rain at the Orchid Creek for the last three days/and at midnight carp come up to the shallows of the rivers." I was inwardly thrilled by the beauty of it all while I observed that my Australian friend remained cold.

You "drink like fish" but we *niu yin* (drink like a cow). One culture's goose is another one's chicken for when you say you get the goosebumps, we say we get the chickenbumps (*ji pi ge da*).

Many years ago I wrote a poem on masturbation called "Birds", beginning with the lines "Playing/playing with the little birds/Between my tree trunks" without realising that in using the word "bird" I was actually unconsciously influenced by the Chinese word *niao* (bird) which is a pun that is lost in English because it is pronounced both *niao* and *diao* (dick), the bird and the dick combined in the same character 鸟 . You have a better word, I think, in "birdie".

Writers: one step higher than beggars

(Yuan Dynasty)

Keeping submerged in English for a time is good as it makes me forgetful about Chinese until I go back to it again. Then, an interesting situation occurs in which I find old familiar words or their usages becoming strange in a pleasurable way, much like my return to China after my first visit to Canada in 1986. I found every woman I met on the street pretty, unlike before when I had thought there were few pretty women in China. Let me quickly come to my point. Last night, in a book I was reading, the author used the expression *sha qing* (kill green) to describe the writing of his book as having been finished. I knew that was the right usage but I was not particularly sure why exactly these two words, "kill" (*sha*) and "green" (*qing*) were put together to mean the end of one's writing process. My dictionary explains it all. In ancient China, people wrote their books on bamboo slips. To protect them from worms and make it easier to write, they would dry up the green bamboo slips before they start writing on them. This process is called *sha qing*, to get rid of the greenness in the bamboo. Now I am really looking forward to the day when I can *sha qing* this book.

American poet Mark Strand wrote a poem, "Eating Poems", that I like very much and translated into Chinese. A Ching Dynasty critic once commented that "reading ancient books is like eating", which I also like.

In English, do we often comment on a piece of writing as something good to eat? Possibly as delicious or delectable? Or tasty? I did come across an Australian review of Zhang Xianliang's novel *Grass Soup* as "unpalatable", which is not unlike a Chinese saying of a writing as so flat that it is *ru shi ji le* (like eating the rib of a chicken).

Years ago a Chinese writer friend of mine said to me that he had a habit of cleaning up his room before he sat down at his desk to do some writing because he would feel as if his mind had been cleaned up that way. A similar reference was made to reading in an article I read today by an early Ching Dynasty critic, Jin Shengtan, who said this of *xi xiang ji* (*An Account of the Western Chamber*), "You must sweep the floor before you read *xi xiang ji* because you can't allow any dust to remain in your chest."

The East and the West seem always moving in opposite directions even when they are trying to merge into each other. Take the speed in writing. The boast a serious Australian author makes to you these days is that he or she (well, actually there's never been a she who told me so) spends at least four years, sometimes even ten years writing a novel. A friend said something to me a few years ago that I can hardly forget. He said, "If a novel does not take four or five years to write, it won't be any good." Well, not for Chinese novelists these days. A famous Chinese novelist told me with pride that he spent only six months doing a big novel. Some would even say that they wrote their novels the first time up and never even revised it or felt the need to revise it again. There is a Chinese tradition of speed writing, though. Li Bai, the Tang Dynasty poet, has a memorable line that goes: *ri shi wan yan, yi ma ke dai* (ten thousand characters can be had on a single day by the side of my horse).

I rose early this morning with the sunshine all over my French window for the first time in many dreary days, and caught this remark on Beijing TV: When they have put up with the slowness of doing things here in Beijing for so long, can they not put up with things getting fast now? I think that serves as a wonderful footnote to what is happening in China in contrast to its past practice of *man man lai* (slow slow come), our version of your 'take it easy'.

I think this will be one of the essential differences between people of letters in the Chinese and the Australian world, that the former will insist on spontaneity and the latter a machine-like precision. The end result: works of uneven qualities akin to God's natural wonders by the former and those of seeming perfection but actual tedium by the latter – for which I reserve no sympathy whatsoever for I admire flawed works much more than multiply revised perfect works of boredom.

Wang Xizhuang's definition of a poet is interesting. He thinks that a poet is not necessarily someone who can write poems but someone who can maintain a detached state of mind and be gentle and cultivated even if he doesn't read or write a single word. I remember going to a reading in Melbourne and seeing this Australian woman poet declaring, in a very exaggerated manner, that she was a poet. I don't know why I felt mildly disgusted but I think I know now.

Ouyang Xiu, the Song Dynasty poet, singled out two lines on poverty for praise. As I like it, I record it here. The poet says that he is so poor that "when I borrow a cart to move furniture, the cart is too big for the furniture".

In English, poverty doesn't seem to be associated with any feelings but in Chinese the word *pin* (poor or poverty) is often closely knit with the word *han* (cold), thus *pin han* (poor-cold) and a word by association: *han shi* (cold scholars). Lovely word. Hu Shi thought that it contains poetry because these *han shi* take pride in being poor and cold.

"Eating soft rice" is an idiomatic Chinese expression that describes a man's reliance on women, particularly for financial support. I find this quite true of today's male writers in Australia.

And as my teeth get worse with age, I sometimes find myself saying to my friends when invited to a dinner: I hate hard rice, please get me some soft rice – only to be laughed at out loud because of the immediate connotation above.

Some people can never understand why people like me can possibly write a book for nothing. Choo, an international marketing manager, has repeatedly asked me over the phone. "But why? Why? Why?"

Marilyn Chin likens poetry to a trade when she says that her struggle as a poet is to "learn my trade". For me, poetry is not a trade; it never is. It is part of my spontaneous life, as cheap as it is and as expensive. And it is, after all, *qi* (air), as I stated before.

In a *qu*-poem written in the Yuan Dynasty, I was intrigued by the poet's comparison of the businessman's profits as tiny as a *ying tou* (fly-head) and a literary person's fame as *wo jiao* (snail's horn). Hence the snail-horn fame and the fly-head profit. Lovely images.

It was only after I came overseas that I heard the common Chinese saying a Taiwanese friend told me. It goes that if you want someone to go bankrupt, the surest way is to get him to run a magazine. That saying took on an Australian flavour when I received a notice from *Otis Rush*, a magazine based in South Australia, that announced its demise by saying, towards the end of the letter, "But it was not possible to keep printing without going to debtor's prison."

Literary fame is a funny thing and, ultimately, boring. The bottom line or top line is the money, to which agents and publishers alike cling.

Yuan Mei complained that contemporary (Qing Dynasty) poets wrote in order to show their learning, their art of composition and their literary inheritance so that their writing is hardly genuine but full of overelaborate formalities, whereas my complaint is that contemporary Australian writing is being produced like a machine, solely for the market.

One thing you never see any Chinese poets write about in their poetry is money but this exception is often made in English poetry. A recent example is Peter Porter who comments on Ted Hughes as someone whose poetry "became more and more a matter of issuing large emotional cheques with no deposits in the bank to support them", something I find hard to accept and wonder if it is the commercialisation of their world that makes their poets so.

Steinbeck says, "America looks on writers as just below acrobats and just above seals." In the Yuan Dynasty, there were ten categories in the social hierarchy, of which the seventh was craftsmen, the eighth prostitutes, the ninth Confucian scholars and the tenth, the lowest, beggars. In today's language, Confucian scholars would be referred to as "intellectuals" or "writers". My feeling in Australia is that writers at least belong to this ninth category, one step higher than beggars, which is why the intellectuals were referred to as *chou lao jiu*, "The Stinking Old Ninth", during the Great Proletarian Cultural Revolution some thirty years ago.

V.S. Naipaul, after winning his Nobel Prize, revealed in public that he had solicited the services of prostitutes. Wang Tao, a well-known nineteenth-century Chinese writer, made no bones about his habit of consorting with whores, claiming that he had "spent forty years among the flowers". To be the lowest of the low, namely, a writer, I guess, one has at least to be honest with oneself, unlike the politicians, the highest of the high, who do it but dare not confess it for fear of political bankruptcy.

A Chinese poet/painter friend phoned me today to say that he is intending to paint some "vulgar" paintings in order to sell for cash rather than keep painting "serious" stuff that no one buys. I said to him that is possible for painters but not for poets because you simply can't write "vulgar" poetry and still sell, at least not to the editors. In this, fiction is more like paintings.

Some literary editors in Hong Kong have a saying that shows a very disparaging attitude towards writers that goes, "It is hard to find 100 dogs but easy to find 100 writers."

Wang Guowei, the Chinese critic who was heavily influenced by Nietzsche, cited four Chinese poets, Qu Yuan, Tao Yuanming, Du Fu and Su Shi to prove his theory that there has never been a case in which great and noble literature can be produced by people without a great and noble personality. I immediately thought of Jean Genet, Thomas de Quincey, F. Scott Fitzgerald and Patrick White, whose writings I appreciate more than their personalities.

I find that sometimes better comments are made in footnotes than in the main body of a critic's work in Chinese literature as in the case of Wang Guowei's book, where in the footnotes a critic is quoted as saying that the difference between Su Shi and Huang Tingjian (whose poems are quoted in Alex Miller's *The Ancestor Game*) is whereas one writes the way a man does when he strides out to meet a guest, the other writes the way a lady does when she takes time dressing herself up and making up before she meets a visitor.

Why do they so care about fame and all that sort of thing, I was wondering to myself, when I was reading this so-called "debate" about a hurt poet's response to a critic's review of his work in a recent review of the *Australian Book Review*. Ultimately, one's worth lies not without, but within.

As soon as I arrived in Australia, I found the so-called academic seminars around the universities here pretty drab. Someone produces a paper. S/he reads it for twenty or forty-five minutes, allowing ten-minute or fifteen-minute question time. I was then wondering why Australians were not capable of delivering lively speeches without any papers as if their memory was lost to the paper. The good thing about Chinese scholars and writers is that there are still a lot (some, I'd say now) who can talk before a large audience off the top of their head. When a country becomes more mechanised and electronised, its people also become more mechanical and electrical, losing their natural abilities as human beings. I, for one, certainly become bolder because I've got a paper in front of me and won't be accused of *zhao ben xuan ke* (reading from the text word by word), a scholarly act that has long been scorned and dismissed in China as mediocre and incompetent.

One Chinese word for "translator" in the past is *tong ci* (through word, like through road), a really nice way of putting it, although, sadly, that has long been replaced by *fan yi* (turner-translator) today.

A professor of English, on reading my English poetry, asked

why I had so many poems untitled. I remember telling him that that was just the way it was, but remained unsatisfied with my answer until recently I read Wang Guowei's *ren jian ci hua* (*Remarks on Ci of This World*). He said that all the ancient poems in *The Book of Songs, The Nineteen Ancient Chinese Poems* and *Ci* down to the Five Dynasties had no titles for the simple reason that "It is not that they do not have titles," he said, "but rather that the meaning in the poems cannot simply be brought out by the titles."

The only reader of poetry is the poet himself. Period.

Poetry has written itself to death.

But professors of poetry are too well paid to be able to write poetry. Instead, they write books on poetry that are very quickly forgotten. Their efforts to buy poetry, however, are well appreciated, if only by the bought poets themselves.

It has recently come to my notice that I read and, of course, write, less and less poetry. In most cases, it is not the poems but the poets that turn me off. I'd wish for a day when poems, unnamed, are broadcast like music so that one could enjoy poetry for what it is, not for who writes it.

Once they assess poetry for award purposes as if it were a commodity, the shelf life of poetry is indicated by "use by".

They don't like the word "vanity publishing" in Australia but that's exactly what the cultural institutions like the Australia Council do in their promotion of Australian literature overseas such as in China by giving money to Chinese publishers to publish Australian books. As far as I can understand from my contact with Chinese publishers, no one is willing to publish Australian books unless they have the Australian dollar first. It is vanity publishing on a national level.

Meeting some Australian writers, I must admit, is really not that exciting. Bakers' Cafe, they say, is a meeting place for

Melbourne writers. I happened to be there on two occasions. On one occasion, I was with a Chinese novelist and an Australian novelist, among others. The Chinese novelist left in the middle of it because she said she had other things to do. The Australian novelist gave me the impression that he was greeting me all the time. Little information was exchanged, to say nothing of gossip or anecdotes. I wonder if this has something to do with the author's fear of accidentally releasing useful but confidential "business" information about their writing.

In 1992, I was invited to a Chinese Literary Festival in Sydney and afterwards we went to a dinner party. At the end of the party, editor of a Sydney-based Chinese newspaper approached me to write a few words on a special page devoted to the festival. I really had nothing to say. I mean I really didn't have the quick wit of some men of letters who could deliver lines off the top of their head as the occasion suits. I happened to remember two lines from a poem I wrote, "Song for an Exile in Australia", which go, "The death of the old world has such weird attractions/while the light of the new world has somehow darkened." I put this down in longhand, much to the delight of the editor and others as something dedicated to the hard-working and hard-living Chinese students in Australia then. Later on, this poem was published in a Shanghai-based literary journal called *shanghai wenxue* (*Shanghai Literature Monthly*), but minus these last two lines. By comparison, when my poem titled, "Fuck you Australia", first appeared in *Westerly*, and, later on, in *Northern Perspective*, neither magazine took out the word from the poem; they did not even change the word "fuck" into something like "f—k". I thought to myself that if I did something similar in China, something like "Fuck You China", it would never possibly be accepted and published, not for the rest of my life and my next life. That does make a difference, doesn't it?

I go to Melbourne Writers' Festival on an annual basis but never buy a book there [I do buy books, actually – 6/1/06]. I don't know why but books there serve as a reminder that people like me will never be published by their publishers, supposedly big. So what's the point of buying?

Censorship is a big headache for any writers, and Australia is no exception. If political censorship is practised in China, economic censorship, equivalent to China's political one, is practised in Australia with an equal amount of gusto and vigilance. The adage you get to hear endlessly these days is: The book is very interesting but we can't take it because of the market! But of course you can't because I know that if it can guarantee sales you will publish anything from toilet rolls to beautifully wrapped-up shit. So much for this sensible crapping. What I initially was trying to say is that the Chinese language offers infinite possibilities to get around censorship. All you do is play the game of the going gets tough and the tough get going. To give you one example, you are not allowed to publish anything with a title containing this expression, *se qing*, literally, colour sentiments or sexy sentiments, but semantically, pornography. However, if you turn the characters around to make it *qing se*, sentiment colour(s) or sentiment sex, then there is no problem whatsoever. A recently published book titled, *Appreciation of Select World Qing Se Films*, is a telling example of this effective linguistic game playing around censorship. Similarly, a Hong Kong based poet called for submission to his proposed anthology of pornographic poetry with a title that contains *qing se*, not *se qing*, without being screened by the Chinese internet guards. In English we don't have to play this game but, well, we end up with a language of less fun.

The difference between Chinese and Australian censorship is that of a parent and a solicitor. The parent takes out the parts he doesn't like without telling you and the solicitor advises you by saying that, "I mean I wouldn't mind you using the word 'fuck' here but it would benefit our readers if you could use 'f—k'."

And, of course, Australians, like their Chinese counterparts, know a pretty word when they see one. Instead of using the word censorship, they say "editing". "This book needs editing," my editors advised. Even if they are the same thing, describing a prostitute as a "service provider" sounds much better than simply say "chick" or *ji*.

There is no censorship worse than not publishing your book.

A short story friend said to me, "Why do you write poetry? I used to write some poetry and soon stopped it because I think fiction is better for a mature man. A poet never grows up."

Does literature have anything to do with illness? I suspect it does. I wrote one of my moon poems as a result of an intense asthmatic attack in which nothing could set my sick mind at peace except writing a poem. An Australian guy who was applying for the same job as I was a couple of years ago in New South Wales put it very practically when he learnt that I wrote poetry. "Oh," he commented. "You did? Perhaps therapeutically?" I hated his way of stripping things down to their core so unromantically but I do admit that he was probably right. When Nick Jose was in Shanghai, I found that he also suffered from asthma. I remember saying to him that asthma seems a good impetus to writing poetry.

You would think that with the aid of a computer and many different kinds of software, the writing business would become much faster and easier. To a degree, yes, but the adverse side of things is that in Chinese set phrases have become so set that there is no turning back. For example, if you type *yi* or "one", the first character of a set phrase *yi guo liang zhi* (one country two systems), you'd get the rest of the characters in no time because they are preset in the software, which means you gain the speed but lose the flexibility because you can't possibly get *yi guo san zhi* (one country three systems) or other possible combinations. Same with other character combinations, a new stereotype created by the Chinese computer, or could it be called "compu-stereotype?"

You say the writer's block but we say *bi zhang* (the pen's obstacle or the pen's block).

Literary prizes are a bore. It's all about fame and money. And the way it makes a person change makes me sick. I make it a rule that I shall never read anything that has won a prize. I only read what I like. You don't eat a fish because it has won a prize, do you?

15

Exile: no cool spring in summer

(Eastern Slope Su)

Some Australians would say, "What do you mean by the West?" whenever I used the term "the West" or "Westerners" in my conversations. Good question. The same thing could be asked them whenever they refer to people from our parts of the world as Asian.

Australia becoming part of Asia? You've got to be joking! Not geographically. Not culturally. It is rather the other way around: Asians becoming part of Australia.

The West is not that individualistic when you come to think of it. Take Australia. Wherever you go, you see the same signs of

McDonald's, Pizza Hut, Grand Hyatt, to just name a few, that come to mind at the time of writing, boring signs of *qian pian yi lü* (a thousand articles written in the one and the same way).

I have lately been thinking of the significant difference between the Chinese culture and the English culture in the word combination, "nation-state", an abstract idea I can never relate to. In Chinese, we would have to say "nation-family" (guo jia), *guo* for nation and *jia* for family, a political term never gone out of currency. Furthermore, every Chinese learner of English knows that when he or she learns the English equivalent to the Chinese *guo jia*, he or she has to learn at least three words: nation, state and country, which are embodied in the single Chinese word, *guo* 国, a square character with four strokes on four sides serving as four boundaries, enclosing a smaller character, *yu* (jade), in its present simplified form or, three smaller characters, *ge* (dagger-axe, an ancient weapon), *kou* (mouth) and *yi* (one) in the traditional script 國, perhaps signifying a weapon defending one single nationstatecountryfamily of mouths. So much for this character analysis and let me quickly come to my conclusion: the learning of English is the beginning of the dismantling of the Chinese (character) as the notion of nation-family breaks up and down, giving way to that of nation-state and that of nation-state-country.

The very reason why Bei Dao, Yang Lian and a host of other Chinese poets keep writing Chinese poetry despite living overseas for many years is perhaps their resistance to allow any languages, including the English, to break their character apart.

This sets me wondering whether exiles everywhere in the world are the same, even in the building structure? Longwood, St Helena, Napoleon's exile, is described as "a collection of huts that had been constructed as a cattle-shed". Now let's refresh our memory of where Chinese intellectuals were banished to live during the Great Proletarian Cultural Revolution: *niu peng* (cattle-sheds).

I suppose being a migrant is being in a state of living with nothingness as an exile, symbolised by the English suffix "less" and the Chinese character *wu*. Which is why in my early poems, consciously or unconsciously, there are so many lines with words "no" and "less". For example, in "Song for an exile in Australia", there are such lines as "knowing very well that **nothing** will come out of it", "in a **poemless** season" and "in a season **without** languages". Interestingly, I found Eastern Slope Su doing the same thing more than eight hundred years ago when he was exiled to Hainan Island where he complained that "there's no meat to eat, no medications for illness, no house to live in, no friends to go to, no charcoal in winter, no cool spring in summer."

In terms of lacunae in one's exile, you would be surprised how similar personalities of various cultures are, such as Eastern Slope Su mentioned earlier, and Napoleon. Living in exile in St Helena, Napoleon is described as "more often than not, doing nothing ... It was easy to see that he no longer had any preoccupation with the future, did not reflect on the past nor care for the present."

Our idea of democracy needs to be shaken up from time to time. I found the division chief quite a distortion who appeared in *Children of the Dragon*, a television serial based on Nick Jose's *Avenue of Eternal Peace*. He acts like a tyrant, bossing people around, giving orders and looking glum. That is anything but a true representation of a Chinese boss that I know of. I used to have sharp arguments with my superiors in China without ever losing my job or anything like that. That is actually an Australian representation because while there are no big tyrants in Australia like Mao Zedong and Deng Xiaoping whose words are the law, there are plenty of small tyrants; to contradict them is to face the danger of losing one's job. That's probably why Nick once said to me, "Australia is basically the same as China." While admitting what he said is true, there is this difference between the big tyrants and small tyrants.

Chinese have willingly washed their own brain of their feudalistic past to such a degree that they are ashamed of mentioning their own emperors and empresses as if they were the symbol of a rotten and corrupted feudalism that must be abandoned in China's progress towards modernism or Western version of modernism. But when I observe the English royal pomposity and display I always wonder to myself why no one has ever accused them of feudalism. Can you imagine restoring a contemporary Chinese emperor to the throne in China now? Go and ask a Chinese.

16

The Ages of Man

(Ovid)

I was interpreting for this client who was about to receive a large sum of money in damages when her solicitor started talking about future income losses in relation, in particular, to her "twilight years", which I found I had no difficulty turning into Chinese, surprising even myself with the phrase *mu nian* (evening years) or even *wan nian* (night years).

Similarly, I rendered another title of a story by a different writer, "The remaining years of the aged Australians", as "The evening years of the aged Australians", the simple reason being your "remaining years" is our "evening years" or "night years".

I know you would describe wrinkles at the corner of one's eyes as "crow's feet" but do you know that in Chinese we describe them as "fish-tail lines" (*yu wei wen*). In my opinion, Chinese are more descriptive and more to the point. My wife did not agree; she said their lines were thicker, which is why theirs were more like crow's feet.

Tonight at www.xys.org, a Chinese website publishing a monthly literary and cultural online magazine, among many other things, I came across an article about the runners of porn sites in China today, who were mostly born in the 1980s. One of them is so young that he is described as a very *yang guang* boy (sunshine boy). I don't think the English language is so flexible and poetic, which is why most of the times I can't read poetry written in English because it's so boring.

I found it easy to translate "As long as his mother's milk was in him a boy was expected to be girlish, a milksop" (*The Whole Woman*), simply because we have in Chinese an expression astonishingly close to it that goes, *ru xiu wei gan* (the smell of the mother's milk not yet dry), perhaps because in both cultures or in all cultures, mother's wet milk in a man is a sign of immaturity.

I seldom ponder the structure of certain Chinese characters and their significance, less still their link to English words, but I recently came across a poet's explanation, or rather, his quotation of an ancient Chinese philosopher's explanation about the Chinese character *wang*, which consists of three horizontal strokes and one vertical stroke going through them, as shown here, 王. The theory goes that the three horizontal strokes represent the heaven, the person and the earth, respectively, but only the person who has a thorough understanding of the three will be able to connect them, like the single standing stroke.

Now, look at the letter "K" that forms the "king". Isn't this "K" also formed of three strokes? And doesn't the vertical line signify the person standing between the heaven and the earth with links to both?

17

Money Swears

(Bob Dylan)

In English we say "money speaks" or "money swears" as Bob Dylan put it. In Chinese, however, we say *qian neng tong shen* (money communicates with God) or *you qian neng shi gui tui mo* (if you have money, you can make the devil turn a millstone).

Do we not have something in Chinese for the expression "cash cows", as described in an *Age* article about the local residents thus treated? We do but we express it differently, of course, calling it a *yao qian shu* (shake money tree), a tree that you can shake to shower money on you.

I came across "splash the cash" today in reading a glossy gossipy magazine about movie stars and their love affairs and I understood the expression at once because there is something equivalent in Chinese that goes, *hua qian ru liu shui* (spending money like flowing water).

It seems that as China is becoming more and more secularised and Chinese people become more practical, their language tends to be less exaggerated than before. At least they don't have to cheer their president Jiang Zeming with *wan sui* (ten thousand years), which was common in Mao's days. In *lao can you ji* (*The Travels of Lao Can*), sometimes translated as *Mr Decadent*, a remarkable novel written by Liu E in 1904, I was struck by his description of his experience in listening to a female singer singing. He said that her voice was so beautiful that all his "thirty-six thousand pores" felt thrilled through and through as if he had eaten the ginseng fruit. I don't think people today would exaggerate things to that degree. Having money in real mathematical terms is far better than having empty figures that sound astronomical.

Great men in China have held money in great contempt. It is said Mao Zedong used deliberately to put the paper money inside his shoes and walked around on them, to show his utter contempt. I came across a similar story in *Sayings of the World in a New Language* of a man who hates his wife's hunger for money and vows never to use the word "money" in his language. To test him, his wife asks the servant to circle his bed with paper money. Next morning when he gets up, he tells the servant to remove "the encircling thing".

"Another day, another dollar", Australians say, just as we Chinese say, *zuo yi tian he shang, zhuang yi tian zhong* (another day as a Buddhist monk, another strike at the bell) but the attitudes shown are very different, almost opposite, the Australian full of capitalist zest for making money and the Chinese just getting along pessimistically and passively.

Although Chinese poetry is so full of mathematics it shuns money or money-related images like death; you'd be hard put to find an instance. Perhaps because Australia is a nation hinged on money, this leaves indelible marks on its poetry. Take Peter Goldsworthy's poem, "Winter Piece", with this line, "the hard economy of winter" and this, "the coins of rain".

Even when we try to be as close as possible, we sometimes still miss. Take "bubble-economy" which translates in Chinese as *pao mo jing ji*, foam economy, not as it should have been: *pao pao* economy, *pao pao* being the "bubble".

When a Chinese describes someone as "generous" he usually means that he is free with his money or with materialistic possessions. I was a little bewildered when I heard one Australian friend describe another person as being "generous" in lavishing praise on him in his review article, in a sense that had nothing to do with material gains. From my experience with both cultures, it really seems to be the case that where one culture is so generous as to give cars or houses as personal presents while the other culture is only so, well, with words.

A recent Chinese expression that gained currency in the 1990s is *xia hai* (down ocean), meaning "to do business" and "to engage in commercial dealings", a metaphor of business as an ocean into which people jump or go down to, a downward movement as against the spiritual upward movement. You wouldn't expect to find an equivalent to this sort of thing in English but you never know. In my translation of *The Whole Woman*, one sentence comes close to the target. It goes, "And they need the money so in they wade".

The Chinese have a word for "swallowing" that I find especially vivid and appropriate for greedy people, which is *jing tun* (whale-swallow), used as a verb, eg. a corrupt official has whale-swallowed millions of dollars.

I am now so used to the unequal equivalents between the Chinese and the English languages that, the other day, when the solicitor said to my client, "He is in their pocket because he would do whatever they wanted him to do" in describing the client's friend as allying with his enemy, I immediately used the Chinese phrase, *chuan yi tiao ku zi* (they wore the same trousers) and saw his face bloom into an understanding smile.

The other day I was in the County Court interpreting for a client about a loan. He was asked by the Judge to state the contents of the IOU and started off by saying "He *jie le* my father ...". Immediately, I found myself in a dangerous situation as I could be found to be making a mistake if I translated it either way as "borrow" or "lend". I was however diplomatic enough to render it to this effect, that he borrowed from or lent to my father etc, and followed it up with an explanation that the Chinese word *jie* means both "borrow" and "lend". Unless the context is specified, the meaning is not immediately clear. This reminds me of what Jiang Zemin, the Chinese president, said when he commented on the Americans' unwillingness to apologise over the recent incident in Hainan. He said something to this effect, that if someone bumped into someone else in the street, the most natural thing for him to say is "Excuse me". But he committed a most common error when he said those words because he should have said "I'm sorry", not "Excuse me", simply because, in Chinese, *dui bu qi*, like *jie*, contains both "I'm sorry" and "Excuse me" and it is an English teacher's hard job to explain when to say which.

Singaporeans do not have this problem when they speak English or Singlish as I noticed in my visit to it a few months ago. A poem I wrote, one of many from that trip, tells of a city "without the passive voice" where they say "Scramble Egg" for "scrambled eggs" and "I'll borrow you a lighter" without ever bothering about "lending" as it happened when I found my lighter missing in a café.

We have *jiao qiong* (cry poor) but never *jiao gui* (cry dear) but I have recently made that (cry dear) a new coinage based on my knowledge of recent arrivals in Australia from mainland China. As five Chinese yuan converts to only one Australian dollar, they find things in Australia much more expensive. As a result, you hear them complain about everything as *gui* (expensive). Hence my coinage *jiao gui* (cry dear). In fact, the first word the son of someone with whom we shared a house many years ago was *gui*. Whenever his parents came back from the market, he would point at something in their plastic bag and cry, *gui*! *gui*!

Nick Jose in a recent *Heat* article on reticence talked about "words that are tainted (perhaps like money) by their currency" which strongly reminds me of a line that the suicide Chinese poet Gu Cheng said. He says that language is like paper money that gets dirtied in daily transactions.

Amazingly, I find a similar remark to Gu Cheng's remark above in a Serbian novel, *Le dictionnaire khazar,* in which the author says that, in my back translation from the original Chinese translation, "Words do not come from the mind and the heart but from the secular and dirty language and foul mouths. For a long time, words have been devoured by the oily mouths and spat out and sucked in by the dirty and foul mouths". I love literatures from "small" countries. In a recent poem, I wrote, the more advanced or affluent a country is, the worse its poetry is written and I think this equally applies to its literature.

"As poor as a church mouse" wouldn't mean much to a Chinese because, for one thing, there aren't many churches in China today and, for another, churches in Shanghai, for example, are full of people on Sundays and are not that poor with fee-paying churchgoers, either. *yi pin ru xi* (as poor as washed) is something Chinese use but I'm not sure means anything to the Westerners. Furthermore, *qiong de tang shi* is a much more vivid one, albeit vulgar, than your church simile. It means one is so poor that one is covered in running shit.

18

Proverbs

(The Bible)

There is a Macedonian saying that goes, “Good friends should always keep good accounts with each other”, which surprisingly echoes a Hubei saying that goes, *qin xiong di, ming suan zhang* (even blood brothers keep clear accounts with each other).

And this Macedonian saying, “No one believes the poor man when he speaks”, is nearly identical with the Chinese expression, *ren wei yan qing* (light person, light words): when a person of little importance speaks, his words carry little weight.

“Gentlemen’s relationship is as light as water while small (minded) people’s relationship is as sweet as honey” is an aphorism my spinster aunt used to make when I wondered about her lack of friends. I would now comfort myself with this from time to time in Australia. And what a lovely image water is here for the gentleman's relationship!

A Chinese folk saying goes that a child "would rather have a beggar mum than an official dad".

And this, too, "Don't boast about what you once were, but speak of how you are now". See how close it is to the Chinese expression *ying xiong bu ti dang nian yong* (a hero does not mention his heroic acts of the bygone days).

Many years ago in Wuhan I heard a woman bus conductor quarrelling with a passenger, telling him to jump to the Yangtze River nearby, saying, "There's no lid covering the river. Why don't you just jump in?" This "lid" thing was brought back to me when I came across this Macedonian saying that goes, "Three things are impossible: a ladder that goes all the way to heaven; a lid that would cover all the ocean; and a human being escaping from death".

I was watching a recent Chinese television serial that ran to thirty-one parts, titled, *The Black Hole*, on DVD, when I heard this expression used, *yin gou li fan chuan* (boat overturned in a ditch), which, reminiscent of the English expression, "storm in a teacup", is different from it in that disasters can happen anywhere in most unexpected places. Still, these two expressions do seem to exist nicely side by side, despite their apparent difference.

And how much is this Macedonian saying similar to the English saying, "Out of sight, out of mind": "Eyes that don't see each other often soon forget each other"? And what about its Chinese equivalent, *yan bu jian, xin bu fan* (when eyes do not see, the heart does not bother)?

"Stinking to the high heavens"? Exactly the same thing as the Chinese *chou qi chong tian* (stinking airs rushing to the sky).

I always remember the "a big fish in a small pond is better

than a small fish in a big pond" expression because I learnt it from an American teacher when he taught us in Wuhan years ago, describing himself as a comfortable small fish in his city. Now, the Chinese have a similar expression, put differently, which goes, *ning wei ji kou, bu wei niu hou* (rather be a chicken's mouth than a cow's rear), meaning that one would rather be the small and clean mouth of a chicken than the big and stinking rear of a cow, with the extended meaning that one would rather be one's own master in a small place than be the servant of someone senior in position in a big place.

I was walking with two friends one afternoon on La Trobe Street in Melbourne when one of them said to the other "once burnt twice shy". Without knowing the context in which he said that, I automatically turned it in my mind into its Chinese version, *yi zhao bei she yao, shi nian pa jing sheng* (once bitten by a snake, ten years shy of seeing a well rope).

And this, "bitten by a snake, he now is frightened of lizards", which matches the Chinese proverb that is quoted above.

The Chinese have a shorter way for "a skeleton in the cupboard", as described in the expression, *jia chou bu ke wai yang* (the family ugliness may not be spread abroad).

I don't know about other cultures but Chinese and English certainly share something in their way of educating their children, in the past if not now. In English you say, "spare the rod and spoil the child", and in Chinese you say (*bang tou chu xiao zi*): "a stick beats out a filial son."

Yesterday I saw a program advertised on SBS about how parents discipline their children with the title, *Loving Smacks*. I haven't seen it but something Chinese say is immediately brought to mind. They say, *da shi qin, ma shi ai* (to smack is adoring and to abuse is loving), an excuse, lame or not, for parents who physically discipline their children.

Ovid is quoted as saying, "Envy attacks the highest, as winds scour mountain summits", which, compared with a Chinese expression, seems pretty verbose. The Chinese expression goes, *shu da zhao feng* (tall trees invite wind).

The Chinese realise that pleasures, as a rule, do not last long and their words show it: *kuai gan* (fast feeling) for pleasure and *kuai le* (fast joy) for happiness.

Confucius says: *xing xiang jin er xi xiang yuan ye.* Han Shaogong rendered it as "similar in nature and diverse in culture". Fine. But what about the measurement words *jin* (near) and *yuan* (far)? I would simply render it as "close in nature but far apart in culture".

To add to what I said previously about my dislike for the English boredom "in the beginning there is the word", an ancient Chinese saying from Wang Xiaobo goes, *ren sheng shi zi you huan shi* (human suffering begins with the knowledge of written characters or words).

In the beginning, there wasn't the word. There was the mouth, the tongue. And there was the penis, the vagina. And there was the mouthvagina, the tonguepenis.

Linda Jaivin in an article discussed the problem of absence of "sex" in contemporary Chinese literature as if it were a deficiency. All I can say is that human progress is not measured by the depth of penile penetration or the width of a vagina on paper.

And to add to the above, I shall quote myself from what I said in a speech I gave to the postgraduates of Wuhan University a couple of nights ago when I noted the major difference between Chinese culture and Western cultures in that sex, for example, is sayable, do-able but not writeable and even if it is writeable it is not deemed publishable for the public. My book of *Western Erotic Poetry in Chinese Translation*, banned for seventeen years and recently published underground, serves as a telling example.

People like Linda need to come to China to experience first hand all the fuckable nights themselves to realise how freely available sex is these days, gaywise or straightwise.

"One lives through worries and disasters but dies in peace and pleasure"; life in Australia as lived by others often reminds me of this Chinese saying.

19

White Peril: *bai huo*

(Kwee Hing Tjiat)

It's probably not known that Chinese are a most colour-conscious race. A popular Chinese saying goes, *yi bai zhe shi chou* (one white covers up ten uglinesses). What does that remind me of in Australia? "Two Wongs do not make a white". I have tried in vain to turn that into proper Chinese and have finally come up with the idea of turning it into something like "Two Huangs does not make a white" (the word "Huang", a common Chinese surname, is "yellow"), and so in Chinese it means "Two Yellows does not make a white".

My uncle, Wang Zheng, is a playwright. When he went to America, he asked me to translate his play, *A Dance for Two*, into English, which I did. As far as I can remember, and this is something that happened about fourteen years ago in China, in one place in the play there is a dispute about the skin of the woman, which a parent regards as dark and thinks should be whiter. When I sent the translation to him I attached a note to the effect that the colour of the skin might be an issue in America. I haven't heard from him since. But "white" is a standard skin colour that most Chinese, ancient and contemporary, hanker for. There is a common saying that goes, "one white covers ten ugly (sights)", as noted above. Interestingly, there are stories about the beautiful white skin colour of Chinese gentlemen in *shi shuo xin yu* (*Sayings of the World in a New Language*). However, it must be pointed out that this whiteness has nothing to do with the Western version of whiteness; it is an aesthetic and poetic, rather than racial colour.

To feel the Chinese passion for whiteness is to daily watch this TV advertisement about a product called *mei bai run fu shuang* (Beautiful White Skin Nurturing Cream), featuring women getting whiter with each use of the cream.

You'd be surprised how the Qing Government in the Qing Dynasty was against racism if I tell you this that, in their times, they'd give a miss to books that contain anti-ethnic minority sentiments, as shown by the ban on the book *shuang feng qi yuan* (*The Strange Serendipitous Fate of the Two Phoenixes*). I mean understandably. If Australia or America was now ruled by a Chinese or a person of other ethnicity, that person surely would not permit anything written containing racist sentiments against him or his race.

Years ago when I worked on my PhD on the representations of the Chinese in Australian fiction, I wrote an article on the abusive language used by Australians towards Chinese and I quoted the lines from a nursery rhyme that go, "Sticks and stones may break my bones but words will never hurt me". I should have known that thousands of years ago there was a similar expression in Chinese that went, in my translation, "Abusing does not shame because it does not bruise the skin nor cause the blood to flow." Was it because of this that those early-day Chinese were able to survive the abusive Australian words such as "Chink" and "Chow", I wonder.

A story for consideration. An Australian interviewed a Chinese guy regarding claims involving a car accident. The Chinese said that because his English was limited he asked a friend for help on the scene. The Australian asked him for his friend's details. The Chinese said he worked in a hospital. The Australian blurted out, without thinking, "He is working there as a cleaner?" The Chinese, hurt, said, "No, actually, he is a surgeon. He has a doctorate in medicine."

Similarly, I attended a conference at the National Library of Australia in Canberra in February 2003 and told my neighbour about it. "Were you interpreting there?" My neighbour was surprised. "No, I was invited to give a paper, actually," I said without any enthusiasm, feeling a little put down, though.

Not long ago there was a report that, according to a study in America, Asians are more intelligent than Caucasians because they excel in academic studies. An Australian professor does not agree, asking by way of a rhetorical question, "but aren't these people Asians who run our restaurants, work as cleaners, factory workers, and do all sorts of menial jobs?" He is definitely right but he forgets one thing: he is talking about Australia where Asians are kept as third-class or fourth-class citizens, by the English language, if not anything else.

When the film *Broken English* was reviewed on SBS, I had expected to see my Chinese actor friends in the film. Not a nose of him or her! There's still a long way to go for Asians to become a significant part of Australian-made films.

In the nineteenth century, "yellow peril" was a frequently used term to denote the fear of Chinese invasion into the Western countries. Interestingly, Lin Shu (1852–1924)[I], one of the most famous Chinese literary translators who translated authors as diverse as Charles Dickens, Rider Haggard and Dumas, without knowing a word of English or French, once translated a work by Haggard in order to teach the Chinese that the white people threatened to devour Africa and then China! It was at this juncture that the "white peril" came to mind but I was disappointed that no such terms were ever coined in Chinese language.

Not true for I've just done a keyword search in Chinese for *bai huo* (white peril). One item returned, among many others, tells the story of a Chinese-Indonesian writer by the name of Kwee Hing Tjiat (1891–1939) who was forbidden from landing in Indonesia by the then Dutch authorities after he published his article, "*bai huo*", in his critique of the Yellow Peril theory.

I often read of Chinese smelling like rice in the old Australian, American and English fiction in which Chinese are depicted in a negative light. However, you might be interested to know what Westerners are depicted as smelling like. In a story by Xu Dishan, pen-named Luo Hua Sheng (Groundnut), a Chinese maid Chun Tao (Spring Peach) works in a whiteman's house but finds her master smelling so foul on account of the beef he eats, the butter he spreads and the milk he drinks that she has to quit. The smell is like it is "issuing from within the pen of the tigers and wolves".

In fiction, Australian or otherwise, written in the nineteenth century, China used to be called "flower land". Interestingly, in contemporary Chinese terms, the outside world, particularly

---

[I] Lin Shu, the rare gifted Chinese literary translator, translated such novels as *David Copperfield* and *Dame aux Camélia*, with the collaboration of Wang Shoucang and Wei Yi by writing down what they orally translated from the original.

the Western world, is often referred to as *hua hua shi jie* (flower flower world), suggesting licentiousness and a tendency to seek pleasure.

In reading a Chinese history of foreign settlement in the mid and late nineteenth century, I realised that foreigners, mainly Westerners, were also identified as "coloured" in those days, revealed by this description that I have not seen anywhere else, *se mu juan fa* (coloured eyes and curly hair).

The stereotype is not a unique Western phenomenon but is found in other cultures as well. The Chinese have all sorts of stereotypes for people from different parts of the country. For example, they have *jing you zi, wei zui zi* (roughly, the oily Beijinger and the big-mouthed Tianjiner) for the glib-tongued natives of Beijing and Tianjin and *jiu tou niao* (nine-headed bird) for the natives of Hubei, part of an expression that goes, *tian shang jiu tou niao, di shang hu bei lao* (as there are nine-headed birds in the sky, there are natives of Hubei on earth). I guess the reason why I say this is that I am a "nine-headed bird" from Hubei myself.

When I told Ali, an Iranian-Australian poet who is also working in Wuhan, in Bluesky Café, a French-run café where I am sitting alone working on this manuscript, he said, "'Poems of a Nine-headed Bird' might be a good title, you know." I suppose so and I might write a book under that title, actually.

People of the dominant race in any nation may discriminate against the ethnic minority people with stereotypes that are surprisingly matching. In a short story by Leslie Zhao, people from Xinjiang Province, a place traditionally regarded as remote and recently viewed as a hotbed for the so-called Eastern Turkestan insurgents, are held in Shanghai as ones who are prone to do *bai dao zi jin* (in with the white knife) and *hong dao zi chu* (out with the red knife). And this image brought my mind right back to eight or nine years ago when my English neighbour made a remark about a Turkish guy coming to my place to show the car that I was intending to purchase. He said, "Be careful with such people. If they are not happy, they'll do this to you." He held up his hand in the shape of holding an imaginary knife and pushed it in the direction of my stomach.

Human character doesn't seem to like the oil, for some reason. In both Chinese and English, if someone is described as "oily", it is not good. In the writings of Edward Dyson, a nineteenth-century Australian short-story teller, the word "oleaginous" is often used to describe the Chinese characters. In Chinese, however, the same quality is referred to with something more than *you* (oily); it is *you hua* (oily and slippery), thus carrying a dangerous element in it as well.

And, in Wuhan, local ruffians are referred to in oily terms as *xiao you zi* (small oily boys).

The Golden West

(Puccini)

The ancient Chinese politician Wang Anshi advised the emperor to "use people of mediocrity rather than people who create difficulties." From what I observe in Australia, that seems the advice followed everywhere although "people who create difficulties" should be changed to "people who have talent" because they are equated with people who create difficulties (meaning trouble) in Australia.

Liu xue (studying overseas) was once not thus called but something else; it was *you xue* (drift-study or float-study). Although this latter expression is now out of currency, I think it captures the spirit of Chinese studying overseas in an important way: they drift from place to place in search of something that they'll never get in an alien country, usually Western and White, where there is absolutely no hope, intellectually.

Ah, well, I should know as I am here, not in Melbourne, but in Wuhan.

An interesting parallel between migrants now and migrants 100 years ago in Australia is the fact that nearly all of them have to do whatever comes their way in order to survive in a new country, sacrificing their own skills, as exemplified by the story of an accomplished French pianist who had to be a labourer in Australia. I have also heard of many Chinese arrivals having to work in factories or other undesirable places lower than their expectations, the way of migrants whether you like it or not. In a play by Ding Xiaoqi, I remember, the protagonist, a former pianist, bursts into tears when he sees his fingers ruined from having done so many dishes in a restaurant! Serve them right, I hear you say. Who asked you to come to our country in the first place?!

Near Christmas time, a writer friend of mine sent me a card, with words to this effect that she had to sell her house in order to *yang jia hu kou*, the expression literally meaning to keep a family and paste the mouths (with food), keeping a family of mouths alive. From this one gets an idea of how hard it is for a Chinese writer to survive in Australia, supposedly a paradise for the workers.

When an Australian talks about security, he is mainly talking in financial terms such as his job, his insurance and his superannuation. When a Chinese talks about security, or rather, safety, he has in mind his political position. An editor, for example, does not publish a piece of writing not because it is not good but usually because its political incorrectness or implications might jeopardise his safety. People lose their jobs for saying something wrong or writing something wrong in China. By comparison, in Australia, people lose their jobs for economic reasons or may we say in Australia politics are economics? I suspect it also applies in other Western "democracies".

In May 2003, I met Ma Jian, London-based Chinese novelist, in Sydney and, over dinner, I asked if he would consider eventually settling in Australia. "Why would I come to the *pi gu*, buttocks, of the world?" he said, in wide-eyed astonishment. That's what I was reminded of when I came across an Indonesian reference to Australia as "the appendix of the body of Southeast Asia".

I don't know about cultural difference but there are certain things a Chinese can never ever share with a Westerner or a white man or woman, which is exactly what I thought of when I read a quoted line by Li Bai the Tang Dynasty poet, who said, *hao yue wei neng qin, liang xiao yi qing tan* (with the bright moon I can't sleep as the great night is good for a clear talk). I know exactly what Li Bai is talking about and have myself had the similar experience of sharing the night with a few friends out in the open. I also know in my bones that this has never happened to me with anyone of European origins and probably will never happen. The moon for me is an extremely lonely one in Australia, a corrupted version of the West, and I'm sure you will probably not agree. Eagerly, I await your response.

Ouyang Xiu had a Taoist friend to whom he sent his own Taoist gown. The friend, after Ouyang Xiu's death, wore that gown for twenty years, patching it up and never washing it, which inspired Su Shi's brother, also a poet, to write a poem. I found this quite similar to Mao Zedong's admirers during the Cultural Revolution when they would keep his cigarette butts or keep their hands unwashed for weeks because they happened to shake hands with him, a typical Chinese way of showing one's admiration and worship. The Western way is simpler. They would auction Ouyang Xiu's Taoist gown and sell it for a large sum of money like they did to Van Gogh's paintings.

Perhaps the most scathing and scatological remark about Hollywood films comes from Wang Xiaobo who says in one of his essays that when you see a lot of commercial films made in Hollywood you are reminded of a "straight bowels country" in the Chinese novel *jing hua yuan*, roughly, (*Serendipity of the Mirrored Flower*). In that novel, due to indigestion, people shit whatever they eat and, to avoid waste, eat whatever they shit, which is possibly recooked with ingredients such as oil and gourmet powder until it eventually looks really like shit. Only then will they have new meals. He goes on to say that the makers of the Hollywood films are cooks of this "straight bowels country" (*zhi chang guo*) and the American audience are the eaters of the shit/meals. I couldn't agree with him more.

A Chinese poet writes: "She is so sublime that I've given up on the idea of committing a mistake" (euphemism for fucking her). Years ago in China I saw a translated film featuring a black man who says, in dubbed Chinese and my English translation, about the Western city he finds himself in: it's so clean that I hardly dare shit!

Gu Hongming, the famous nineteenth-century eccentric, was often taken to task in England for his weird "backward" tastes in relation to the bound-feet and other things but he always had something to say in retaliation and in his defence. When questioned why the Chinese men liked to smell women's bound-feet, he said that the English regarded toe-dancing (ballet dancing) as the pinnacle of their art. The only difference between that and the Chinese liking for the tiny feet is that the English reserve their dancing toes for public watching while the Chinese keep the small feet for private use. He then went on to say that the English habit of "binding the waist" of their women was even worse, as it would cause the whole body to distort and degenerate. Again, when asked why the Chinese liked to smell the feet, he retaliated by saying it was just like the Westerners liking to eat the stinking cheese and smelling the stink before eating it. So, it was all an "art of smelling", he said.

A recent example in Wuhan of something similar table-mannerwise. When Westerners complain that Chinese eat with too much noise one observant Chinese remarks that he is horrified by the Western habit of blowing their noses with such a noise that it sounds quite frightening and, more disgustingly, they wrap it up and pocket it.

Ouyang Xiu, a famous name-sake literary man of the Song Dynasty, opened his famous essay, "An Account of the Pavilion of the Drunken Old Man", with a very short line consisting of only five characters, *huan chu jie shan ye* (Encircling Chuzhou city are mountains, or Chuzhou city is encircled by mountains). The well-known part of the anecdote is that the sentence alone went into several drafts until it was reduced from more than a dozen to only five characters. Stephen Owen, the Harvard Professor of Chinese literature, translated that into very bad English as "Encircling Chu-zhou all around are mountains" in his latest anthology of ancient Chinese literature from its beginnings to 1911. But Henry Lawson's writing has this Chinese quality of terse succinctness when he opens his "The Drover's Wife" with "Bush all around". I don't know why Americans miss the point. For myself, I'd rather re-translate that opening sentence as, "Chuzhou. Mountains all around".

We have now gone past the Age of Information and entered into the Age of Information Rubbish. While I'm writing this, my wastepaper basket is full of promotional stuff from Telstra, the Folio Society, the Softback Review, the *Reader's Digest*, and the banks, all so glossily and colourfully printed. The other way to deal with such rubbish as the standard commercials on TV is that as soon as you hear "we'll be back", you say to yourself "I'll be back, too" and then go away and make tea or coffee or go to the toilet to piss or simply read a few paragraphs from the book you are reading until the program comes back on again.

Sadly, something similar to this "I'll be back" adage is followed on every Chinese TV channel today, breaking the flow of programs to an annoying degree.

Jiao qu translates into "suburb" but does not really carry the same meaning. When Nick Jose introduced the idea of the great Australian suburbia to us in Shanghai, we had very little idea of what that meant. For me, I was living in a Wuhan suburb; a suburb in a Chinese metropolis provided easy access to the green wheat fields, rice paddies, village fishing ponds and roads that branched into small towns and other cities. The notion of maddening quietness and inhumanity of an Australian suburb is alien to any Chinese used to the suburban life in China. Without understanding this difference, it is futile to just match the words.

This, sadly, has also changed as Western-style villas spring up everywhere in the suburbs of Wuhan so that a woman editor once said to me by email a couple of years ago: We are similar now!

If I say Australia is much less multicultural than China, few here would agree with me. Let's just take literary translation as an example. Few, if any, well-known authors in the West have not been translated into Chinese in big volumes. You name it: from Ernest Hemingway to Henry Lawson, from William Shakespeare to Frederick Schiller, from William Golding to Patrick White. It is not exaggerating to say that Chinese children grow up with this Western "spiritual" food. Chinese literary landscape or windscape had so long been multiculturalised that

I thought it is part of us. It is people, rather than the sort of "spiritual" food, the real thing, that multiculturalise Australia.

Westerners and Chinese must have a different concept of beauty, at least in regard to their view of Chinese women. I remember a scene many years ago in which I asked the group of Americans for whom I interpreted to choose who they thought were the best-looking women among the girls serving us in the restaurant. For some reason, they invariably chose the worst-looking girl, from my point of view. Reading a short story by an American man recently, I came across this reference to an American woman as "high-cheekboned beauty", which set my teeth on edge. In Chinese terms, the high-cheekboned women are not regarded as beautiful. The Americans must have different eyes from ours, I must say.

As if to prove this point, a writer friend of mine told me when I visited Yunnan that an "ugly" woman in his workplace who could not find a boyfriend for years was eventually "handpicked" by an Australian and went with him to Australia!

Single-lidded eyes and double-lidded eyes. Does that make sense to Australians? If it doesn't, it does to most Chinese. A male classmate of mine went through an operation many years ago to make his single-lidded eyes into double-lidded ones. Chinese novelist Zhu Wen wrote a story titled, "Single-lidded Eyes, Double-lidded Eyes", in which the main character wonders if he can find any single-lidded eyed girls on the street nowadays because "double-lidded eyes, like big breasts and big buttocks, have become an inseparable second feature of women", swept by a "globalised wave". In an attempt to Westernise themselves, I should add. How sad! How interesting! How stupid! How clever! But one thing is true, that a single-lidded eyed culture is being lost in favour of a double-lidded one in the Chinese self-colonising process.

Mind you, though. There is a similar trend, on a minor scale, that has been quietly going on here in Australia. A few years ago I met a Queensland-based white woman who was surnamed Tan but had no Chinese in her family. I have since forgotten all the details of her story except her happiness in getting rid of her "boring" (her own word) English surname once and for all.

About a week ago I went to a party with some of my Chinese friends and noticed, among other things, that the daughter of my friend seemed to have grown prettier than before till I was informed by my wife that she had recently had an operation in China to make her eyes double-lidded. Self-colonisation in a nutshell!

This is a phenomenon no longer surprising as I have taken quite a number of digital photos of Chinese boys and girls who have dyed their hair in yellow or pink on the streets of Wuhan, Beijing and Shenzhen.

To put it in simple terms, the Chinese *yin* and *yang* means the "feminine" and the "masculine", apart from their many other derivative meanings. Perhaps it is not insignificant that the Chinese call their own calendar *yin li* (the Yin or Lunar Calendar) and the Western calendar *yang li* (the Yang or solar Calendar). In a way, they have inadvertently feminised themselves and masculinised the West, showing a long tradition of worshipping things Western, as indicated by the *mei guo* and *ying guo* above.

Leslie called me the other day. He always calls me when he comes back to Australia once in a while. We were talking about the Western obsession with Chinese politics, their illogical and detached concern for the Chinese lives and their wrong notion that as a writer living in China you do not have the freedom to write. "Well," said Leslie, who, an Australian citizen, has chosen to live and write in China. "You still have to live in China." Quite irrationally, the word "sky" emerged in my mind, perhaps as a result of my having been thinking of it and its related implications over the previous few weeks. Living under a sky you can't hope to change it no matter what. Is Australia that perfect? Is America? Is any other country? It is always easier to focus on other people's pain and one's own pleasure. So much for this political thinking but the expression that followed from there is *tan tian*, the Chinese equivalent to the English chat, chatting or chit-chatting. Word for word, though, it is "talk sky".

Many contemporary Chinese terms that have arisen as a result of increasing contact between China and the world are difficult to turn into English because there isn't the equivalent. For example, one term I frequently heard people use in China in late 1995 and early 1996 is *yu guo ji jie gui*, meaning "to get onto international rail track". Whenever they talk about newly built freeways with their roadway signs and so on, they use this expression. When they talk about cultural and literary matters, they also use it. But I find this not easy to turn into English. And it never seems to work the other way, though, that is, the West never seems to want to *jie gui* with China.

The upshot of this *jie gui* (connect rail and, in my coinage, connect devils, for *gui* for rail sounds exactly the same as *gui* for devil) over the last decade is that now China buys the copyrights from the West, to the tune of 50,000 titles per year, whereas it manages to sell only 2000 titles to the West annually. I got the information from a publisher only yesterday (7/1/05).

A Ching Dynasty poet once wrote that "poetry benefits from the assistance of the rivers and mountains". That set me wondering about Australian landscape where there are no impressive big rivers and tall mountains and the longer I live in Australia the further away I find my own poetry is moving from the rivers and mountains into the domestic environment, a theme that would be regarded as trivial and unpoetic by most Chinese poets although the ordinary has now become a major theme for the younger Chinese poets.

Rivers and Mountains: on literature/nature connections

(Qing Dynasty)

I was in County Court doing an interpreting session when the barrister I worked for observed that Chinese language was very natural or nature related, such as the way we refer to the Aboriginals as "the earth people". When I come to think of it, it is certainly true that our language is often nature related. Take wind. Our word for landscape is *feng jing*, which means "wind-scape", not something you can own, like a piece of land, but just like a wind. The ancient expression for the poet is a *feng ren*, "a wind person". I don't know how this comes about but it says a lot about the nature of a poet. Then, there's the word *feng liu* or "wind flow", actually meaning many things, from being a great personality to being lascivious and flirtatious or even gallant. Then, we describe gossip as *feng yan feng yu*, that is, "wind words and wind language", which will make a good title for my next book of poetry if it is not good for anything else. Still, I like words like wind, once said, twice blown away.

Words are winds or else why do so many Chinese words have wind in them? For the English "risk", the Chinese word is *feng xian* (wind risk). For "style", it is *feng ge* (wind pattern). For "rumour", it is *feng sheng* (wind sound or get wind of something). Wind bone or *feng gu* means the strength of character and wind taste or *feng wei* is the local colour. The English are not that imaginative with winds and tend to be vulgar; you only have to hear them "make wind" to be convinced of this.

What do you say when you go to the country to collect folk songs? Not anything specific? Well, I'll tell you what we say: *cai feng* (collecting wind).

Does "fish-belly white" (*yu du bai*) mean anything to you? If not, you are not Chinese. It is a generally accepted description of the daybreak or the dawn when there is a line of daylight shown on the horizon. Hopefully, with my introduction, this long-existing expression will come into currency in English.

When the vice-governor of Hubei Province was put in jail for corruption, he said that he "loved *jiang shan* (rivers and mountains) and also *mei ren* (beautiful women)". Now *jiang shan* means the state power, which is why the Chinese say *da jiang shan* (fight for the rivers and the mountains, or strive for political power). It would be unusual for a native English-speaker to talk about the state power or a piece of literary writing in natural terms but this has been part and parcel of the Chinese linguistic and literary tradition, used on a daily basis without people even realising that they are resorting to metaphors. Take *jiang hu* (rivers and lakes) in a poem by Zhong Dao, in which he says "man is floating in the *jiang hu*/how can he not bring a knife?" For Chinese, this *jiang hu* is never meant to be taken at its face value or its face word (refer to the earlier chapter in this book). It is a place outside the control of the government officials; it is the gangland; the green woods of Robin Hood; the place where all the underclass gather, including the poets, as indicated by the title of a novel written by Yi Sha, *jiang hu ma tou* (*A Wharf in the Rivers and the Lakes*). Part of the Chinese poetic tradition is the so-called *shan shui shi* (mountains and water poetry), to which we don't seem to have anything similar in English poetry. In describing what he thinks is the best way to write poetry, Su Shi, commonly known as Eastern Slope Su, said that it should be something like "moving clouds and flowing waters, of no fixed features, that move when they feel like moving and stop when they cannot but stop". Qian Zhongshu, when criticising Huang Tingjian, another Northern-Song Dynasty poet, for his obscurity, resorts to natural terms, saying that his "language is not transparent enough but is like the windows in winter covered with a layer of steam and frozen into a spread of icy flowers". Do Australian critics ever talk about their subjects in these terms? Not that I can readily think of. One term, though, that has come into the English language is *feng shui* (wind and water) but the other one, most commonly used in Chinese, has not, which is *feng liu* (wind flow), meaning, among other things, dissolute. Even the political is the natural, to the Chinese. For example, recently, European and American influences in China are referred to as *ou feng mei yu* (European winds and American rain).

I was just about to wrap this up when I came across a critical article in Chinese in which the essays by a writer who has contributed to *Otherland* are described in purely natural terms that go, "Liu Liangcheng's abilities lie where he can put all his words in a clearly bright and transparent creek and wash them until each one of them is clean."

It is not till I played an Australian music CD for my students that I realised that, actually, just as there is mountain and river poetry in China, there is also mountain and river music in Australia. The CD *Daintree Dreamtime* by Ken Davis, which I brought back from Australia, is full of running creeks and mountain birds, something they have never heard before.

Probably one of the best examples for literature/nature is the Chinese euphemism for lovemaking, which is *yun yu* (cloud and rain) although this has gone out of currency in contemporary writings.

Nan ti shan, a male-body mountain, is what I came across in my reading for the first time in a Japanese novel translated into Chinese although I have seen many describe mountains like women's breasts. And it is also in this novel, *shi le yuan* (*Paradise Lost*), by Watanabe Junichi, that I saw a woman's private parts referred to as a "garden that quickly moistened" [my translation]. A lovely image.

In another instance, the moon is an often used image for literary activities. A literary man of the Qing Dynasty, Zhang Xinzhai, once remarked that "Reading as a teenager is like peeking at the moon through a slit; reading as a middle-aged man is like enjoying the moon in the garden, and reading as an old man is like watching the moon on the balcony."

The thing is that, for the Chinese, nature isn't simply nature but something more. Often it represents their moral character. The old images that men and women of letters like to use include the "four treasures" or "four gentlemen", which are *mei lan ju zhu* (the winter plum, the orchid, the chrysanthemum and the bamboo) and the bamboo, the winter plum and the pine are also known as *sui han san you* (three friends in a cold winter).

You can't kill time but you do, in English, and we can't *sha feng jing* (kill landscape), but we do, in Chinese. If someone does something that kills landscape, he dampens your spirit.

When Zhang Xianliang was here a few years ago I asked what he thought of Melbourne. He said it wasn't much different from any other European cities he had visited. Same style of buildings. Same coloured people. But the thing he objected to most was a visit to a friend's farm in the country; he literally hated the country. It is not so surprising considering that he has spent more than twenty years in a Chinese labour camp in the Northern Wilderness. Landscape, whether it is Australian or Chinese, means the same to him: the labour camp.

When Lillian Ng is quoted as saying "Mountains and rivers are easier to alter than a man's or a woman's behaviour" in Alison Broinowski's book, I suspect it has been turned around to suit the English speakers or readers as this involves two instances of reversal. First, in Chinese, we say *jiang shan* (rivers and mountains), not the other way round. Second, in this particular saying, well known to all Chinese, it is not people's behaviour that is harder to change but their nature. Hence *jiang shan yi gai, ben xing nan yi* (it is easier to change rivers and mountains than the nature of people).

And, of course, the poet Lin Bu's description of *mei qi he zi* (having winter plum as my wife and cranes as my kids) is a rare example of nature as part of one's moral character.

Compare that with the title of a poem by John Shaw Neilson, "The crane is my neighbour", and you'll find how similar is this idea of having nature as one's partner across cultures.

What do we say when we want to convey the idea of too many conferences or meetings or official documents? I have no idea, but the Chinese description, *wen shan hui hai* (mountain [of] documents and ocean [of] meetings or, simply, word for word, document mountains and meeting oceans) seems an apt one.

I could never understand the "sea change" until one day when I was hit by the Chinese expression, *cang hai sang tian* (sea and mulberry fields), enormous changes symbolised by the sea turning into mulberry fields and the mulberry fields turning back into sea.

We do have something that comes close to "sea change". It is "sky change" or *bian tian* (a change of sky), although it often carries a negative connotation, e.g., a change of the political regime.

A Chinese critic notes the nature-related pen-names of some Chinese poets when he points out that putting nature in their names shows that they still regard nature as "the spiritual resting place" in their hearts. Quite possible but I would have thought that is just because the Chinese poetry is so oriented towards and centred upon nature down the centuries that the Chinese poets have been conditioned to this conceit. Just look at their names: Xi Sai (West Frontier Fortress), Xi Chuan (West River) whose real name is Liu Jun (Army Liu), Zi Di (Purple Land), Hai Zi (Ocean Son), Ge Mai (Dagger-axe Wheat) whose other pen-name is Song Xia (Pine Summer), Mai Mang (Awn of Wheat), Xiang Zi (Acorn) and Ouyang Jianghe (Rivers and Streams Ouyang), a conceit that Western literatures with a much shorter history have yet to adopt or perhaps to ignore.

One thing Liao Jingwen says perhaps explains everything about the link of poetry and nature. He says, "The beauty about poetry is that it is aided by mountains and rivers," and he supports this statement with anecdotes of how poets of various dynasties wander in search of poetry by the rivers and in the mountains.

Eastern Slope Su writes so many beautiful poems about the lake, the mountain, the birds, the river and the moon but he never writes a single poem about the sea. The lack of poems about the sea in ancient Chinese poetry is appalling. Actually, when he was on his sea journey to Hainan Island, Su described himself as a person whose "heart was dazed and soul lost". I guess this fear of the sea is what eventually brought China to the feet of such sea-faring peoples as the English, the Portuguese, the French and the Japanese who had many poets writing about the sea.

The literature-nature connection went back to *The Book of Songs* (1122–256 BC), one of which about a woman goes thus, *shou ru rou yi, fu ru ning zhi, ling ru qiu qi, chi ru gua xi* (her hands are like soft young cogongrass, her skin, congealed fat; her neck, the young longicorn; her teeth, the seeds of the gourd).

Ruan yu wen xiang bao man huai (an armful of soft jade and tender fragrance) is a line from an anonymous poem but it gives you an image of a man holding a woman in natural terms.

Lang (wave) as a Chinese word means more than its English counterpart "wave" can ever match. There once was a novel titled *lang shi* (A History of Wave), which was actually a book of pornography because of the associations of the word *lang* with its protagonist "Lang Zi" (wave son or wave gentleman). In another context, *lang zi* means "prodigal, loafer and wastrel", possibly because of the movements it necessarily involves, one rolling after another, like waves. Alex Miller makes good use of this expression by naming one of his main characters Lang Tse. On a trip to Hainan Island, a tour guide told me of a *shun kou liu*, constructed entirely on the word *lang* or wave: *er shi bu lang san shi lang, si shi zheng zai lang jian shang, wu shi sui lai lang da lang*, all because he happened to catch a glimpse of the big waves rolling as our bus went by the seaside. The whole thing means, if anything at all, "If you do not *lang* in your twenties, you'll *lang* in your thirties; when you reach forties, you reach the peak of *lang* and when you are in your fifties, you *lang* after *lang*." *lang*, used as a verb or noun, here means "loose" or "dissolute".

Meanings are translatable but multiple meanings contained in a single word defeat attempts at translation. For example, Wang Guowei singled out two words that he thought were particularly effectively used in two different poems. The one is the word "noisy" in the line, "the spring is noisy on the branches of the red plum tree", and the other the word "play" in the line "as the clouds break the moon, the flowers play with their shadows." However, the word "noisy" cannot even bring out one tenth of its original flavour in Chinese and the same is true of the word "play" simply because there is nothing in English that is entirely equivalent to these two words that contain many hidden meanings in the original Chinese.

Sky flower or *tian hua*. Beautiful, isn't it? Until you know what it means, that is. In Chinese, it means smallpox. And what about pain wind or *tong feng*? Nice combination, ha? Well, it refers to gout; a friend of mine is currently suffering from it, the pain wind.

The mouth is still associated with the river when it comes to eloquence or nonsense in Chinese. Hence *xin kou kai he* (his mouth talks casually as if a river is opened up) for talking nonsense and *kou ruo xuan he* (he talks as if he has a river hanging from his mouth) for eloquence. By comparison, the English language is so colourless and boring. What is more striking, to an English-speaker, is that these are not pretentious expressions but are part of daily oral discourse, something a Westerner will find hard to understand.

Sometimes, direct translation seems the only way to produce immediate impact, the meaning coming later. A Chinese writer friend of mine who has very limited English once did this with the Chinese expression, *ren shan ren hai*, producing very humorous effects when he said, People Mountain People Sea. Which is an exact copy of the Chinese expression. In the dictionary, this expression is given an unfortunate explanatory definition as: "a sea of people". I like People Mountain People Sea much better. What about you?

Do we say high summer in English? In Chinese, we have high autumn, although it is differently phrased as I encountered in this poem I was translating today. I thought the best way to render the phrase *qiu gao qi shuang* was through direct translation which makes it "autumn is tall and the air is crisp". Now I could have turned it into "autumn is high and the air is crisp" for the same effect, or even "the air is crisp in high autumn". Either way, it is better than the dictionary definition that makes it "the autumn sky is clear and the air is crisp".

There's much that is similar between the expressions related to the bandits in both Chinese and English culture. For example, when the English say "go to the greenwood", the Chinese describe people having done so as being the *lü lin hao han* (good men of greenwood).

An interesting thing in Chinese is the word combination of "the bandit" as it consists of the two words "earth and bandit" in *tu fei*, as if they come out of the earth. And if someone becomes a bandit or earth bandit, he is described as *luo cao*, fall grass (fallen into the grass).

In early 2007 I experienced *luo cao* in Xiapu, Fujian, China, when I fell drunken into the grass and over a cliff, nearly killing myself. My poet friends ever afterwards refer to it jokingly as my "*luo cao*" experience.

I've recently finished reading Wistawa Szymborska's *Poems New and Collected: 1957–1997*, and I must confess that I don't really like much of it. However, one line about the Aborigines has some relevance to my book as it refers to them as "sprouting up as if from the earth itself". Did she know that the Chinese word for Aborigines is *tu zhu* (earth people)? Probably not.

President Robert Kennedy was turned into *ken ni di* (chewing the muddy ground) in the 1960s China. Transliteration, by comparison with translation, is easier if you are careful with its negative or positive connotations. This is what I did in translating the Aboriginal word "corroboree" in *Capricornia* when turning it into *ke le bao ni* (can please you until you are full, or, in plain English, filling you with pleasure).

Beat His Chest: *yi pai xiong pu*

(Liu Guande)

Hu Changqing, vice governor of Jiangxi Province, recently executed for his corruption and economic crimes, was known for his extravagant lifestyle and for boasting about it. Once he pointed to his leather shoes and said to his entourage, "You know what these shoes are made from? They are made from crocodiles' leather. They are worth more than 3000 dollars. Have you ever seen them before?" You know who he reminded me of? Two poets. One is Robert Creeley whom an Australian novelist told me about more than ten years ago in China as making a similar remark about his expensive leather shoes. One Chinese poet also told me about another Chinese poet who, on coming back from overseas, could hardly conceal his pride in his newly bought leather shoes. Sometimes one's shoes reveal oneself more than one's hats, it seems.

Have we heard of government officials being referred to as "fathers and mothers"? Well, *fu mu guan* (father and mother officials) has long been used to refer to those officials who lord it over people.

Years ago, I gave Mou Qizhong in China a telephone interview from Australia for a film-related research project on the millionaires in the world. I remember he was saying that, despite his multi-million-dollar businesses, there was only so much he could eat on a day-to-day basis. He is now in prison but not because he ate little. In reading *The Summing Up*, I liked Somerset Maugham for what he says about himself as a person with "enough plain food to satisfy my small appetite". These days, however, some Chinese I have met give me the impression that all they have got is huge stomachs and dicks with insatiable desires.

English is a very verbal language, much more so than Chinese. However, there is an expression in Chinese that uses rare verbs for which there is no match in English. For example, *yu rou ren min*, which translates as "to fish and meat people", gives a vivid image of how the rich and the powerful can lord it over the poor and the weak by eating them as "fish and meat".

I know what *gu ming diao yu* means and I know you don't. Still, when I came across it in a Chinese translation of a book written by a French-Chinese, I made a comment in the margin that there's no equivalent to it in English. What it means, word for word, is buying a name and fishing (one's) fame, possibly because of this ancient story of Jiang Taigong who fishes with an empty hook day by day and year by year until he gets noticed and invited back to the royal court as a general. I was surprised that I was proven wrong when I checked it in a Chinese-English dictionary where the expression is given the definition, "fish for fame and compliments" but I prefer my own version.

They say in English a "name dropper". We do have this kind of people in real life but our language does not reflect it. Our closest equivalent to that is *diao shu dai* (dropping the book bag) or a "book bag dropper", which refers to someone who likes to show off his learning either in his daily talk or in his writings by constantly making allusion to the books he has read.

I have never been able to find the English equivalent to the Chinese *da guan qiang* (beating the official tone or speaking in an official manner) until I came across "power talk" in my newspaper readings.

It is a pity that cultures tend to sacrifice invention for the mere sake of understandabilities. *Big Wrist* (*da wan*), a film by the mainland-based director, Feng Xiaogang, is a case in point. When it was released in the West, it was titled, *Big Shot's Funeral*. There's nothing to criticise about the title because you have to make it easily understandable to an ignorant Western audience. The point is, however, Big Wrist has become so synonymous with being big shots or big bosses in China today that I was amused to read a woman refers to herself as a *wan* (wrist) of some sorts in the same book mentioned above. Personally, I'd rather opt for a bit of cultural shock at the expense of my understanding than tolerate stupid stuff like "big shots" for it is narrow-mindedly parochial and provincial, not big-wristly enough for my liking.

It would be scarcely logical to describe a spiritual leader as a spiritual *ling xiu* (collar and sleeve) but *ling xiu* (collar and sleeve) as an expression denoting leadership has been used for a couple of thousand years in Chinese. I guess why I mention this is because my dad once commented that one's collar and sleeves were the dirtiest places on a person.

Sometimes it is surprising how connections can be made between poets of very different times, places and nationalities. More than a thousand years ago, Su Shi alias Su Dongpo or Eastern Slope Su wrote in one of his most famous *ci* poems, "Prelude to the Melody of Water", that "I'd like to return riding the wind/but I am frightened of the crystal palace and the jade tower on high where I might not be able to stand the cold". Hence *gao chu bu sheng han* which roughly translates in contemporary Chinese daily language as "higher up, I cannot stand the cold" and which also implies that the higher up one is in official position, the more danger or isolation one faces. John Ashbery has a line in his poem "How Much Longer Will I Be Able to Inhabit the Divine Sepulchre ..." that goes: "But where in unsuitable heaven/Can he get the heat that will make him grow?" Though this strongly smacks of the flavour of the line by Su, it does not have the contemporary overtone the Chinese line has.

In translating *My Fortune in Australia*, a Chinese novel, my collaborator and I had an interesting problem reaching a compromise about a Chinese expression. In one place, to show that he is full of confidence, the main protagonist *yi pai xiong pu* (beat his chest or chest-thumping), a gesture one makes when one feels confident, in Chinese or China. However, my Australian co-translator points out that the gesture has to turn into something different in English, like "puffing out his chest" to make sense because "beating one's chest" might suggest self-pity in English.

There is an interesting addition to this chest-thumping in a local Wuhan expression that goes, *ma ma pe zhong liao,* in Wuhan accent, as taught me by a local friend. *Ma ma* means "the tits" on a man. *Pe zhong liao* means one beats his chest (tits) so much that they swell up as a result, suggesting someone who boasts without doing anything.

You say "bottom line" and we also say that, *di xian*, but we say something you don't, *di qi* (bottom air). The expression, alive on the living Chinese lips, has yet to find its way into any official Chinese dictionaries but it means the basic strength one must have in order to achieve something.

In English you say "winner takes all". In Chinese, we say, *ying jia tong chi*, "winner eats all".

How would you describe an ignorant or uneducated person in a simple English phrase? I don't know but the Chinese expression is there, ready for the taking, *xiong wu dian mo*, which literally means there is not a single drop of ink in that guy's chest.

In my recent visit to San Francisco while attending a conference there, I met someone whose father's name is Wu Wo, which in Chinese means "without me" or "I-less". Nothing surprising, as the state of being I-less is one of the highest any cultured or literary person would try to achieve in Chinese culture. Even the Chinese grammar shows this: a sentence can begin without the subject. For example: "raised my head to watch the moon/lowered my head to think of my home" (from a poem by Li Bai). However, it would make little sense when translated into English, whose culture puts so much emphasis on the importance of being I, being an individual; even "I-less" sounds like "eye-less". Who would want to go eye-less or I-less?

23

God

I remember John Steinbeck's *Of Mice and Men* came originally from Robert Burns' "The best-laid plans o' mice an' men/Gang aft a-gley" but that's only because I was reminded of this by a well-wrought Chinese way of putting it, *ji hua bu ru bian hua* (no plan is as good as change, or you can't plan for change). And that sets off a further comparison between the English "man proposes and God disposes" and its Chinese appromixation, *ren suan bu ru tian suan* (man's calculation is not as good as heaven's calculation).

For your "man proposes but God disposes", we have something similar but more mathematically effective: *ren you qian suan, tian you yi suan* (man calculates a thousand times but heaven calculates only once). And that "heaven calculates only once" could very well be turned into a title. Ask me for it first, please, before I use it.

I'd like to stretch it a bit. Just as the word "mental" is directly related to the mind, so God has something to do with its Chinese counterpart *shen jing* (mental), as the character *shen* means God. Which is probably why most Chinese mental patients I have encountered always have the name of God on their lips.

Gao Xingjian, in his novel, *One Man's Bible*, says, "You have written this book for yourself. This book of escape, your personal bible. You are your own God and your own saint" [my translation], which has a more vulgar version in one of Yi Sha's poems, in which he claims that he is his "own Dad".

Religion is, after all, a way of life, and, for some probably a better way of life. When I got myself into trouble with the school authorities in a university many years ago, a friend constantly urged me to take on Christianity, saying if you keep praying to God things will take a turn for the better. That has never worked for me so far. God is actually yourself.

24

Pleasure/Pain Principle

(Sigmund Freud)

I've never realised that the Chinese word for pleasure is actually synonymous with pain until I saw the title of a story published online in a Chinese literary website, *tong bing kuai le zhao* (painful and happy). For the Chinese word for happiness *tong kuai* (pain pleasure) or *tong tong kuai kuai* (painpain pleasurepleasure) means exactly that, "pain-pleasure". While Westerners as a rule try their hardest to separate two different ideas from each other, Chinese have a habit of combining them, perhaps from their firm belief that these two things are one and the same and better so than separated.

When Germaine Greer says that "Penetration of a tight dry

vagina causes pain but pain can become indistinguishable from pleasure", she is redundant. In Chinese, the word for pleasure is a two-word combination, *tong kuai* (pain-pleasure). Maybe it's not her problem but the English's.

If you say "it pains me to see or do something", it makes perfect sense. But if I say his mother *teng* him (his mother loves him), *teng* in Chinese meaning "pain" as a verb, it would make no sense, would it? In fact, *ai* or love is sometimes combined with the word *teng* to form the expression, *teng ai* (pain-love), used both as a verb and noun. Perhaps, only love with pain is genuine love; anything short of that would be less.

The mainland Chinese version of the English "AIDS" a few years ago was *ai zi bing* (disease of love) until it was surreptitiously dropped in favour of a more blameless one of *ai zi bing* (disease of moxa). Pronounced exactly the same, the *ai* in this case meaning nothing or anything from the "moxa" to "fine" and "stammering". In Singapore, as I later found out, *ai zi bing* was given a more amusing twist as to mean the disease of love.

In translating a Chinese poem about the terror of ordinary daily life, I came across this expression in Chinese, *mao gu song ran*, *mao* standing for "hair" and *gu* for "bone". Without thinking, I rendered a direct translation of it as "the hair and bone terror" in the last line so that it reads "it is in this hair-and-bone terror that they wake up". In checking the English-Chinese Dictionary, I find a number of definitions under the entry, *mao gu song ran*, that go "with one's hair standing on end – absolutely terrified" or "be bloodcurdling". Well, I think I like my direct translation better as it retains the image of hair and bones.

Sometimes, the Chinese language is so illogical that it allows "hair and bone" to be used not with terror but with pleasure, *xi huan de mao gu song ran* (hair and bone pleasure), as in *The Nine-tailed Turtle*.

Sweat in any languages may suggest fear because fear induces sweat in us. However, when you say "in a sweat", we say *nie yi ba han* (holding a handful of sweat), usually for someone else if you are concerned for his or her safety.

Last night, the English Department celebrated the end of the term with a huge dinner in which I got half drunk and, at the same time, I was sweating profusely. A friend commented: "that is good because it means you are a good drinker, everything evaporated through your sweat." Which reminds me of an old friend's mother who could drink any men under the table because everything she drank tended to be evaporated through her sweat; all she needed was a rag to mop it off under her armpits.

Cooking the Telephone Porridge: *bao dian hua zhou*

(Cantonese)

I don't remember where I came across the word "feast" but when I did on the cover of a glossy magazine about clothes I received a shock. The word seemed to solve one of the puzzles I had had for a long time over why Easterners in general and Chinese in particular were so addicted to food. Even the word "feast" itself contained "east" in it. And for some reason, when I looked at it, it just stared out at me, demanding my attention to feast my eyes on it.

Can we sum up one culture with one single word? If we can, then "sex", or "fuck" in its secular form, can be used to describe English or English cultures and *chi* or "eating" can be used for

Chinese culture. In Chinese, you can eat anything, even surprises (*chi jing*). Their word for "suffering losses" is *chi kui* (eating losses). You can eat medicine (for taking medications) and, by extension, you can eat regret medicine (for being regretful). There are many other examples of a similar kind but a recent expression based on Cantonese dialect is *bao dian hua zhou* (pot-cooking the telephone porridge), pot referring to the Cantonese style of cooking porridge with earthen pots on a slow fire, the description of a situation in which people have long telephone conversations as if they are pot-cooking the porridge over the phone.

Perhaps as a result of this eating influence, Australian-English has one expression not found elsewhere: Let's eat Chinese.

In my October visit to Beijing, a local poet talked to me about a phenomenon with writers and poets in China. Once a writer or poet produced something very good, even if it was a book or a single poem, he or she would "eat it" for the rest of his or her life, a case of one-bookism or one-poemism that could last one a lifetime. The only thing that I can "eat" more than a decade seems to be *Moon over Melbourne and Other Poems*. First published in 1995, its second edition has been released in the UK and its American edition will be out soon although I do not know how much longer I can "eat" it after that and there isn't much to "eat" out of it, really. I now recall Jim's referring to poems as a kind of bank deposit: a poem you wrote years ago ends up being included in an anthology and then finding its way into a school texbook, thus keeping you paid continuously over the years.

Idioms thrive on the things we eat. As with the porridge, so is the rice. The lack of rice-related idioms in English equals that of pudding-related idioms in Chinese. I remember "the proof of the pudding is in the eating" being translated in Chinese as "the proof of the pear is in the eating", or, more closely, "if you want to taste the pear, you'd have to eat it", a case of one language's pudding is another language's pear.

Skip the pudding and I shall show you a random selection of rice-generated phrases and expressions in Chinese. *Fan tong* (rice barrel) for a good-for-nothing; *fan dian* (rice inn) for a hotel; *fan lai zhang kou, yi lai shen shou* (when the rice comes, the mouth is opened, and when the clothes arrive, the arms are extended), an expression about lazy people content with being fed and clothed; *fan keng jiu nang* (rice pit and wine bag), a reference to someone who only drinks and eats without doing anything; and "rice bowl", one's employment.

I was working on the translation of a book on tattooing when I thought of translating something "forbidden" as *jin guo*, forbidden fruit. Then I changed my mind as I remembered our equivalent, *jin luan*, forbidden meat. But that's where the similarity ends for the English forbidden fruit is biblical whereas the Chinese forbidden meat is royal, going back to more than 1600 years ago when Sima Rui, before becoming Jin Yuan Di Emperor (317–313), had to give the meat of a pig above its neck to the emperor because it was delicious. Hence forbidden meat reserved exclusively for royalty.

One of the things that often set me wondering in my first few years in Australia is the nonchalance people show towards the ripe plum trees in summer. In early summer, you often see trees lit up by the delicious brightness of the plums that ripen until they drop, unnoticed. At first, I'd pick them up and eat them. Later, like most Australians, I get so used to them as part of the summer scenery that I don't even touch them. Then I read this story, again from *The Sayings of the World in a New Language*. Here is it in its entirety [English translation mine]. "At seven, Wang Rong often wanders around with other kids. When they see the plum trees by the roadside have plenty of plums that break the branches, they scramble for them except Rong. Asked why, he said, 'If the trees stand by the road and still bear many children, the plums must be bitter.' Those who pick up the plums then realise how right he is."

One word that I find hard to translate into Chinese is "raw". Sometimes it is a praise to call a piece of writing "raw" in English. However, it is hard to render it into right Chinese as the Chinese word for "raw", *sheng*, means life itself, being alive or live, most often used to describe the uncooked, meat or otherwise. Besides, being "raw" would give an impression that it is uncouth, unpolished, even rude. I now have a better idea since that day in Beijing when I rang a poet friend to check if he had received a copy of my underground published novel, *The Angry Wu Zili*. He said yes. And I asked if he had read it. He said yes, with a single comment, "It's *sheng meng*." "How do you mean?" I thought I heard it wrong. "*Sheng meng*!" he said. "Don't you even know what that means?" Of course I do. It's a word often used in the restaurants to describe the lobsters, especially the Australian ones, commonly known as *ao long* (the Australian dragon [lobster]), normally best eaten raw. This character-combination means alive (*sheng*) and ferocious (*meng*). As a matter of fact, I think it would be best-suited for "raw" in translation and I applied it in a piece of translation not so long ago for the Melbourne Symphony Orchestra.

By the way, the Chinese do eat lobsters uncooked, meaning completely raw, the flesh but not the shell. We call it *yi xia san chi*, one lobster, three ways of eating: first, eat the meat inside, raw and uncooked, then have the bones fried and the rest of it made into a soup.

My mother, when she was still alive, used to describe my two brothers as *cai long cai hu* (dish dragon dish tiger) for they would devour any delicious dishes like dragons and tigers. I used the expression in anticipation of a friend coming to dinner yesterday with his son as I knew from my past experience that the two, like my two younger brothers, had a dragon and tiger appetite for anything we served them at home. But of course, my use of this expression was only well intended without any malice and we had to be prepared.

Food is never related to disasters in Chinese as it is in English. See this: a recipe for disaster.

One's language is conditioned by one's culture. Sex is so pervasive in Western cultures that you can find loads of sex-contained words such as fuck, dick, dickhead, pussy, etc. In Chinese, eating is the thing. As the Chinese proverb goes, *min yi shi wei tian* (food is the sky for people). Hence many eating related words. To praise a piece of literary writing as good is to describe it as *kuai zhi ren kou* (minced meat roasting one's mouth). To say someone is daring or foolhardy is to say he must have *chi le bao zi dan* (eaten the leopard's gall). To describe someone as erudite is to say he is a *bao xue zhi shi* (a scholar who has eaten his fill of knowledge). One other example is *hua bing chong ji* (drawing cakes to allay hunger), which means to feed on illusions.

We don't just eat vegetables and meat; we also eat landscape with its beautiful scenery. Hence the phrase "feasting one's eyes on". The Chinese, well known for their gluttony with regard to food, adopt a similar approach. They say, *xiu se ke can*, when they see a beautiful piece of landscape or scenery. This phrase, translated word for word, means "Beautiful colours (of scenery) can be eaten for a meal."

Chinese table manners have changed considerably in recent times. One sign is that no one seems to care any more about chewing noisily as my parents strongly cautioned against in the olden days (the 1960s and 1970s). The other is the way in which people don't clink their glasses while making a toast these days. Instead, they hold their glasses and hit their bottoms against the table in front of them to acknowledge *gan bei*, bottoms up, quite a lazy and effective way, similar to that employed by an English academic in the recent conference in San Francisco that I attended. He patted the table in front of him with open palms to make a noise instead of applauding with his hands like everyone else. Similar also to a lot of people here in Melbourne at poetry readings where they might simply make an applauding noise by patting their thighs or anywhere that could make a noise.

Relaxed and Comfortable

(John Winston Howard)

This morning when I went to the city, I saw two people going the rounds collecting coins from parking meters, one collecting from the meters and the other putting them in a box, then locking it up. My memory went immediately back to the late 1980s when I was in Canada: the delegation had a rule that no one was allowed to go out alone at night; at least two people had to go out together. What a pair of mutual supervision! The difference, though, is the former is political and the latter, economic.

I was reading this article in today's *Age* about love between employees in a corporate environment, with the forbidding message "your relationship or your jobs!", when I recalled what was happening in my university days in the late 1970s and the early 1980s in China. Back then, the student card bore the message that love was not allowed between university students and, worse, if two classmates of opposite gender became friends, the university authorities would make sure that they were separated by assigning their work in provinces far apart from each other, say, the girl in New South Wales and the boy sent to the Northern Territory. Still, that analogy would be lost on ordinary Australians as, after all, you can come back to Sydney if you can't get used to living in Darwin or vice versa; you couldn't in those days if you lived in China.

John Howard's slogan "be relaxed and comfortable" has recently found an echo in the Chinese novel, *li hun shi dai*, that I've just finished reading. The successful people are described there as those men who are married but have mistresses outside their marriage and they talk in no haste, no hurry. That's the current Chinese version of the Australian "relaxed and comfortable" if you want to know.

In the book *A Place in the Sun*, John Howard, the current Australian prime minister, is said to have "made the bullets and Pauline Hanson fired them". When I read this, a similar Chinese expression came to mind, "using someone as a gun", which would have been used in a similar situation in Chinese, where it could have been more easily said that, "John Howard has used Pauline Hanson as a gun."

I thought *cao min* (grass people) is something ancient but could not locate it in *Ocean of Words (ci hai)*. However, it immediately reminded me of the English "grassroots", a word that is not found in contemporary Chinese vocabulary although widely available in the overseas Chinese press and some published Chinese articles here.

When we say "as poor as a church mouse", do we know that

the Chinese have a term for the poor? They call them *qiong guang dan* (the poor bare eggs), similar to the Australian "poor bastard", as I found in an Australian poem.

Whenever Australian politicians talk about ordinary people as "battlers", my mind goes blank until I recall the Chinese *lao bai xing* (the old hundred surnames), a wonderful match for the Australian battlers. Same with the "diggers" as a reference to Australian soldiers, for which the Chinese match, as I found it, is *zi di bing* (sons of the people's army).

Like the wolf smoke, *huai rou* is also an expression no longer in use, a political reference to the feudal rulers making a show of conciliation to bring other nationalities or races or states under control. When a Sydney-based Chinese writer described multicultural policy in Australia as one of *huai rou*, I became intrigued, not by her description of it as such but by the strange meaning of the word-combination: *huai* for holding something in one's arms and *rou* for something soft or softly. Hence holding something soft in one's bosom or holding it softly, a more apt description of sex than politics. An image of many different cultures held in the bosom of Australia springs to mind, a little incestuously, reminiscent of a documentary shown on SBS some years ago, titled *The Embraced*, on how the Chinese students were being embraced by Australia.

When I was little I read a lot of the so-called *xiao ren shu* (small people books), the picture-story books, but one of the few things I can still remember is a scene in which a Western army was launching an attack on the Chinese army with an army band leading the way so that the band became an easy target for the Chinese fire. We found that hilariously funny and stupid of the Westerners. However, there is another detail in a similar Chinese situation that I can recall, in which the Chinese soldiers, all martial artists, rushed out towards the enemies armed with the most advanced Western weaponry, half naked and holding swords in their hands, while shouting war cries, *dao qiang bu ru! dao qiang bu ru!* (Sword proof! Bullet proof!), dying by the dozens. That is the Chinese stupidity on a gigantic scale, I thought. When I come to contemplate this again in Australia, I find that I can understand both sides perfectly. Few in the world can beat the Chinese in their emphasis on the cultivation of the human body to the degree in which it is supposed to be proof against any attack by any weaponry whereas the West has such a strong belief in the power of music that it seems it is all they need to defeat the enemy with.

The Chinese expression, paper tiger, used by Mao Zedong to refer to all the Western imperialists, has now found its way into the mainstream English language, evidence that you have to be famous enough for words to travel acceptably from one language into another. I know I'm being facetious again but in the English borrowings, they never know that alongside the paper tiger, we also have a most often used expression, *xiao mian hu* (smiling faced tiger or, simply, smiling tiger), that describes a person with a wolf heart but a smiling human face. Or, in your terms, a street angel but a house devil.

Another well-known Chinese expression that has paper in it is hardly ever known in English: *zhi bao bu zhu huo* (paper doesn't wrap up fire), meaning truth will out.

On a couple of occasions, I saw on television snatches of how a newsreader read the news on North Korea's television: he or she read it with downcast eyes, strikingly similar to one Chinese newsreader on National television straight after the June Fourth Incident in 1989. But I wonder if that is a result of their anger or discontent or fear.

I Like Chinese

(Monty Python)

You'd think porcelain or china very fragile but do you know the Chinese word for solid is composed of china by combining two characters *ci* (china) and *shi* (solid)? Hence, *ci shi*, china solid. It's really a combination of two opposing or conflicting ideas but it works! The very nature of Chinese word-combinations, in a way. Or perhaps of Chinese nature as well, soft on the surface, firm inside?

Chinese people (of the mainland extraction) do have an inventive sense of humour in creating taxi-related expressions. Apart from the commonly used *da dee* (beat a taxi), beat meaning take, they have *da mo dee* (beat a motorcycle taxi), *da ma dee* (beat a foot-pedalled vehicle taxi that vibrates so much it makes you feel numb or, in Chinese, *ma*), and, more recently, *da huo che dee* (beat a train taxi) from a poem by Yi Sha, and *da bo yin dee* (beat a Boeing taxi) from a rich guy who jokingly referred to a Boeing airplane as his own taxi!

Interestingly, my recent reading of some online Chinese material has brought my attention to this phenomenon in another dimension, namely, the so-called "political mathematical autocracy" which shows how obsessed my countrymen or ex-countrymen are with expressing themselves in literary and political mathematical terms. Cun Yi, author of an article in *China Monthly*, an online magazine, points out that Chinese leaders from Mao Zedong to Deng Xiaoping were wont to resort to mathematics without any accuracy, not even any reason, such as when Deng says "Our policy on Hong Kong will remain unchanged for fifty years". Cun Yi questions this by saying, "Why not forty-nine years or fifty-one years? Where did he get this notion of fifty years?" Similarly, Mao said in the 1950s that China would "catch up with Great Britain in fifteen years" and that, to get rid of illiteracy, every Chinese must "learn 1500 to 2000 characters", which Cun Yi refers to as a fortune-teller's way of dealing with major issues of a nation. This reminds me of a story, hearsay of course, that I heard years back in regard to the common practice of adding and subtracting a zero by the media. Whenever something bad is reported, such as a political demonstration, a zero will be removed from the total number of demonstrators, reducing 10,000 to 1000 whereas if something good gets into print, one zero will be thrown in, thus the average individual income of 1000 yuan a year may become 10,000.

Many Chinese idioms consist of four characters with numbers from 1 to 10, for example, *yi qiong er bai* (one poor two white), abject poverty; *yi mu shi hang* (one glance ten lines), reading very fast; *san qi si qie,* "three wives and four concubines"; *san fan wu ci*, "three times five occasions", many times; *san san liang liang*, "in threes and twos" (see the order in reverse?) *san yan liang yu* (in three or two words), equivalent to the English "in a word or two" (see the reduction?); *si fen wu lie*, roughly, "divided into four or five pieces", a fragmentary state of affairs; and *si ping ba wen*, roughly, "four steady and eight stable", description of a person of stable personality; *wu hua ba men* (five flowers eight doors), varied; *wu yan liu se* (five colours six hues), multi-coloured; *wu guang shi se* (five lights ten colours), multifarious; *qi zui ba she* (seven mouths eight tongues), all talking at once (compare this with "I am all ears"); *qi pin ba cou* (seven rig up eight piece together), piecing together; *qi shang ba xia* (seven up eight down), being agitated; *ba jiu bu li shi* (eight or nine not far from ten), nine out of ten; *jiu niu er hu* (nine bulls two tigers), exerting tremendous effort; *jiu niu yi mao* (a hair out of nine bulls), a drop in the ocean; *jiu si yi sheng* (nine deaths one life), a narrow escape from death; *shi quan shi mei* (ten complete ten beautiful) for being perfect and *shi you ba jiu* (ten has eight or nine) for nine out of ten. Now, that's ten out of ten. And, mind you, ten is not really the best for when a Chinese is extremely happy, he is not just 10-point happy (shi fen gao xing); he can be 12-point happy, even 120,000-point happy, the "point", I suspect, originating from the 10-point scoring system in international sports competition or vice versa.

"Give me five!" When an Australian asks me to do that, I can't form that in Chinese because we do not have an equivalent, not even the necessary gesture to accompany it in our culture. The nearest thing that comes to it is: hit the palm. There is the expression, *he shi* (combine ten) but that's a gesture of Buddhist greeting by putting the two palms together. Even the Cross is not the cross but a *shi zi jia* (character ten frame), the Chinese character 10 being 十.

One of the difficulties in translation into Chinese is contemporary English words such as "cool". I was presented my doctorate at a ceremony held at La Trobe University when the old vice-chancellor asked me how long I spent in finishing the PhD thesis as he handed me the certificate. I said, "Three years." He whispered into my ear, "That's cool." Afterwards, I spent a long time mentally trying to translate that into Chinese but in vain because literally it wouldn't make any sense in the same situation in Chinese. The Taiwanese translation, a Taiwanese friend told me, is better than I can ever imagine. The word in Chinese is pronounced *ku*, which means cruel but in a cool way because of the association of its English equivalent in sound and meaning. I happen to come across a comment on ancient Chinese poetry by a Ming poet, who puts poetry into many different and, in my opinion, odd categories. He says, "It is easy to write cool poems but difficult to write hot poems, easy to write obscure poems, but difficult to write fine [as in weather] poems, easy to write quiet poems, but difficult to write busy poems, easy to write poor [as in poverty] poems, but difficult to write rich poems, easy to write low poems but difficult to write noble poems, not because poems are difficult to write but because quality poems are difficult to write." I like this connection of the postmodern and premodern. In fact, the Western postmodern is the Chinese premodern. I wonder why contemporary critics do not introduce new critical terms like cool but use trite critical terms like resilient, poignant, lively and all that meaningless jargon.

Last week, I finished my first term as professor at Wuhan University with a lecture on gay and lesbian writings in the Canadian and Australian Chinese diasporas and in contemporary China. In the list I provided my students, I included some terms for gays and lesbians in China. For gays, we have *tong zhi* (comrades), a term that came into currency about two decades ago, and, for lesbians, we have *la la* (pull pull), a word that may have originated from the word "lesbian" with its "le". The most offensive term for gays is *gao ji de* (men who do G or the G-doers), "G" as the letter that stands for Gays.

When you come to think of it, the English language is actually a much more exclusive one than the Chinese. While it allows occasional creeping in of other languages, including the Chinese and the Japanese, it hardly ever accepts the existence of characters, Chinese in particular. However, the contemporary Chinese language is full of Chinese-English hors d'oeuvres, according to an enraged Chinese scholar who dubs the English language the *ying yu ya pian* (English Opium) as part of the "Cultural SARS" in China. Without getting too theoretically complicated, I can just tell you that in a 183-character Chinese passage there are twenty-one English acronyms, from a newspaper article, such as WTO, MBA and IT. It has come to such a pass that the Chinese have taken up a similar practice by becoming more phonetic instead of character based. Some examples instantly come to mind: TMD (fuck his mother's), JB (dick) and PF (admire), all because TMD stands for *ta ma de*, JB for *ji ba* and PF for *pei fu*. Such a new language is becoming unstoppable especially online and in writings by the generation brought up on computer screens.

The English language is threatening to become the "English SARS" in China, as Zhu Luzi's book *The Devilishly Possessed English* makes amply clear. However, one of the benefits for the younger generation is that they can freely use English words in their Chinese writings, sometimes inventively. In *Abandoned Love Letters* by Mu Zi Mei, notorious for her practice of inviting men to fuck her and posting writings about her love-making scenes online the next day, achieving millions of hits daily, she writes in a mixed English and Chinese way, posing a question to herself: How many men have you "happied" with? (36). In her writing, it's not even "happied with" but, simply, "happy".

English may claim to have a vocabulary close to 500,000 words but that's only because it collects everything that Chinese declines to collect, willing to be second only to English in vocabulary while retaining the largest number of speakers. But for the elitist Chinese lexicographical tendency to include only the most recent and the most relevant in commonly used dictionaries, we would have been able to see words in translation from English that were current 100 years or so ago, such as *kang bai du* for comprador, *na mo wen* for Number One and *hong mao hua* (red-haired speech) for English. Many words, originally translated from English, have become so Chinese that few even know that they are foreign any more, such as *ju le bu* (club), *kang nai xin* (carnation) and *sha fa* (sofa).

The Chinese language becomes more creative with the introduction of English, leaving English behind, slow to catch up. One example suffices. The word "bar" has now been turned into the Chinese "ba" for *wang ba* (internet bar), *jiu ba* (wine bar), *qing ba* (clear bar, clean bar and, actually, pub) and even *yang ba* (oxygen bar, another name for the anion air-cleaner), the last such a nice description that a poet used it to refer to the open air on a public square.

One aspect of contemporary Chinese language is its inventively adverbial use of words, particularly with the younger generation. For example, a girl can be described as wearing her jeans very "westly" (in a western manner). Before she had a leg (sex) with her boss in his house, her boss very "leaderly" asked her to sit down and very "leaderly" asked how he could help her. This unusual description helps capture the cool way in which the young, aggressive women of today depict the men of their sexual consumption.

Chinese culture often stresses the balance, rather than

extremity, of things, such as *tian di* (heaven and the earth), *ren chu* (people and animal) and *hao huai* (good and bad), etc. In the sixteenth century China, as one Portuguese traveller noted, the locals had a way of causing a male bird and a female bird to sing to each other by putting them in two separate cages and easing the drudgery of grinding a mill by putting one blind person on either side so that they might talk to each other while working or resting.

In retrospect, there are times when the culture is not so balanced. For example, Chinese has the expression, *mai chun*, selling the spring (prostitution), but not the opposite, *mai qiu*, selling the autumn.

In English we say, "seek high and low" whereas in Chinese that would have to be "seek up and down" (*shang xia qiu suo*). It almost seems as if our sense of directions is entirely different from each other, reflected even in our description of a person's height. While you say how tall he or she is, we say how high; in my hometown, people even use *chang*, long, to describe the height of a person. This makes me wonder if the Chinese language is inherently more poetic than the mundane English.

It is perhaps the difference between points of view. Take the uneven bars. I suspect it's this centric and correct tendency on the part of the English speakers that makes them use the "even" as the starting point of measurement. Anything that deviates is "uneven". By comparison, the Chinese take a poetic view because they look at the bars like it's a piece of landscape with mountains in it. Hence high and low bars (*gao di gang*).

Likewise, you say horizontal bar while we say *dan gang* (single bar); you say parallel bars while we say *shuang gang* (double bars).

Sometimes, we, I mean Chinese and English, are very close in meaning except for the image. For example, when I translated the sentence in *Capricornia* where Mrs Shay spoke "in a cracked voice" on seeing Norman Shillingsworth for the first time after sixteen years' absence from Port Zodiac, I had a range of words to choose from: husky, hoarse, broken, and broken-gong, the last being a common expression in Chinese for people who say things in "a cracked voice", like someone talking in a voice that sounds like a cracked gong. For effect and imagery, I settled for the gong, knowing very well that it may sound like something else when back-translated.

Equivalents: *yan juan*, sick tired

As soon as an Australian says, "I'm sick and tired of" something, I realise that this is probably the only phrase that ever matches the Chinese word for word, for *yan juan* is just that, "sick tired".

The tall poppy syndrome is not unique to Australian culture. In Chinese, this is evident in one ancient poetic line that goes, *mu xiu yu lin, feng bi cui zhi* (if a tree stands pretty in a forest, the wind will destroy it), and, of course, in the recent expression, *hong yan bing* (red-eyed disease) as well as the old expression, *qiang da chu tou niao* (shooting the bird that sticks out its head).

In both English and Chinese, there is the expression about

eating one's words, the Chinese being *shi yan* (eating words). However, the other Chinese expression, *shi yan er fei* (eating one's words to get fat), is yet to find its way into English.

In the courts, the magistrates court or the county court or other courts, where I do interpreting jobs, you often hear the judges or the barristers reject some evidence by referring to it as "hearsay". When you turn that into Chinese, it becomes bulky. It becomes *dao ting tu shuo* (road hear path say).

Likewise, in these two languages, there is the expression "laughing stock" (*xiao bing* in Chinese), but the Chinese have one more expression *hua bing* (talking stock).

You say "homesickness" but we say *xiang chou* (homesadness or villagesadness).

Whenever I see the sign, "Liquorland", I am reminded of the Chinese expression, *hua tian jiu di* (flowery sky and liquor land), a life of debauchery.

Hail, Poetry

(W.S. Gilbert)

Shi hua (poetry remarks) is an ancient Chinese form of criticism that aims at picking out the best lines of one poet and talking about their beauty in comparison with other lines of poetry by other poets of different historical periods. Instead of writing wordy articles that can be put into anthologies or collections later on as writers are wont to do these days, poets in days-gone-by would say a few words about what impressed them most in their reading and say no more. Lately, consciously or unconsciously, I only read Chinese books, going backwards until I hit this book titled, *shi hua and xiao pin from Previous Dynasties*, *xiao pin* being small, sketch-like articles. In an attempt to learn from my Chinese predecessors, I recorded my impressions as briefly as possible, for no one else except myself, for the contemporary West remains blind to the gems of the ancient Chinese literature in its ceaseless pursuit of wealth and fame and conquest. I beg to be excused for not putting in any reference to the time and place of these poets and their poetry. Mine is only for the intelligent and learned and, ultimately, for myself.

Su Dongpo or Eastern Slope Su once wrote a line that goes, "I've had enough of everything in my life/Except for my want of death"(*ping sheng wan shi zu, suo qian wei yi si*). I suppose he could say that because he had at least been a high official in the government, a well-known poet and, what's more, had a concubine.

I don't remember if any Chinese poets, ancient or contemporary, ever write "shit" into their poems. Mao Zedong is an exception. In one much-publicised poem written late in his life, he says, *bu xu fang pi* (Stop farting!), which translates nicely into "Bullshit!" Yi Sha, my favourite contemporary Chinese poet (not any more though by now, June 2003), is of course another exception. In a poem that I like but find hard to translate, titled "Song of Childhood", he ends the poem with two lines that he learnt as a kid, "a great flood in the toilet = shit surging forward" and "throwing grenades into the shit holes = bombarding the people's shit".

One thing that watching *Rush Hour* in which Jacky Chan plays the leading role reminded me of is "found objects". As painters do with them, Chan plays his martial arts with "found objects", humorously and dexterously, such as chairs and sofas, just whatever lies within his reach.

Westerners' pursuit of fame and colonisation is reflected in the personification of the places, e.g., Melbourne, Sydney, Wellington, Washington, Vancouver and Paris. The Chinese naming of their places is an extension of their poetic imagination, e.g., *chang jiang* (the Long River or the Yangtze), *huang he* (the Yellow River), North Capital (Beijing), On the Ocean (Shanghai), Fragrant Harbour (Hong Kong), West Peace (Xi'an) and Martial Man (Wuhan).

The latest reversal from Australia: my agent emailed me bad news today about an Australian publisher who refused to consider my new collection of poetry. I was not surprised because that guy had never published a single word by me and had been known as someone who always refused to publish any writings by Asian-Australians until I raised the issue with him a few years ago. He has since brought out a couple of books by AAs (Asian-Australians) although I am permanently removed from his list. I did not know that my agent would approach him or else I would have stopped her straight away with a Chinese expression: I know you will *peng dingzi* (hit the nail) with him. Then it dawned on me that the Chinese 'hit the nail' is not synonymous with the English 'hit the nail (on the head)' as by 'hit the nail' the Chinese mean 'bumping one's head against the nail'.

"Poetry kills but we'll kill it before it kills us" popped in sight when I opened a poetry website. I forgot which. But I was reminded of it when I came across a line by Huang Canran, a Hong Kong-based poet, who wrote, "In the bosom of poetry is hidden the motive of killing." What a coincidence! And this is a poem dedicated to a poet who died young.

In the history of Chinese literature, Yuan Dynasty is criticised for its poetry that is too much concerned with trivialities that happen around the poets and men of letters and centre round poets who write for each other. Now, when I read this I can't think of anything more like it than the contemporary Australian poetry, so much of it bearing names of the poets who are friends, for which I never have much time.

You can send or mail a letter but when a Chinese says *ji yu* it is so poetic you are tongue-tied to translate it except directly: "to mail reside". In fact, to *ji yu* is to live away from home, like something mailed to a residence far away, a human being contained in a letter, living the life of being mailed.

When a Chinese writes about someone living in this world but with a feeling of almost *chu shi* (going out of this world), he expresses an admiration for that as if it was the perfect state of things that could ever happen to a person: living both in and out of this world.

Bibliography

All translation to English of the Chinese titles is mine unless otherwise specified

The Australian Review of Books, October 2000.

Ah Wu, "*mao hua lian pian*" (The cat's unceasing speech). *Hong Kong P.E.N.* June 2000, p. 171.

An Dun, *jue dui yin si: dang dai zhong guo ren qing gan kou shu shi lu* (*Absolute Privacy*: An actual oral account of the feelings of the contemporary Chinese), New World Press, 1998.

Anonymous, "*nü ren dou shi ye ti*?" (Are women all liquids?), *aohua shibao* (*The Australian-Chinese Times*), 4/10/01, p. 16.

Ash, Susan, "An Uncertain Elsewhere: Foetal Imaging and Maternal Narratives", *Salt*, Vol. 15, 2002, p.1.

Ashbery, John, *Can You Hear, Bird*. New York: Farrar, Straus and Giroux, 1995.

Baihua, *wang qi de ren* (*The Man Who Watches the Air*). Taipei, Taiwan: Tonshan Publishing House, 1999.

Billingsley, Phil, *Bandits in Republican China* [trans. Xu Youwei et al. as *min guo shi qi de tu fei*]. Shanghai People's Publishing House, 1992.

Boyle, Peter, *What the Painter Saw in Our Faces*. quoted in *Imago*, No. 3, 2001, p. 193.

Broinowski, Alison, *About Face: Asian Accounts of Australia*. Carlton North, Vic: Scribe Publications, 2003.

Brown, Rebecca, "Trying to say", *The Literary Review*, Vol., 46, No. 3, 2003, p. 439.

BuzzWords, No. 11, April, 2001, p. 32.

Casule, Ilija and Thomas Shapcott (trans/eds), *An Island on Land: Anthology of Contemporary Macedonian Poetry*. Macquarie University, 1999.

Celan, Paul, *Poems of Paul Celan: revised and expanded* (trans. By Michael Hamburger). New York: Persea Books, Inc, 2002 [1972].

Chang Yao, *chang yao de shi* (*The Poetry of Chang Yao*). Beijing: People's Literature Press, 1998.

Chen, Fang et al. (eds), *dang dai liu xing yu* (*Popular Contemporary Language*). Beijing: China Social Publishing House, 1999.

Chen, Guangxing (ed.), *wen hua yan jiu zai tai wan* (*Cultural Studies in Taiwan*). Taipei: Chuliu Book Company, 2000.

Chen, Jitong, *zhong guo ren zi hua xiang* (*Les Chinois peints par eux-mêmes par le Général Tcheng-Ki-Tong*) [translation based on the 5th edition in French, 1884], translated by Huang Xingtao et al. Guiyang: Guizhou People's Publishing House, 1998.

Chen, Jiaqi, "*wen ge hua yu guan kui*" ("A peek at the discourse in the Cultural Revolution"), in *Thinking*, No. 2, 1996, p. 284.

Chen, Liping, *"chun jiang hua yue ye"* ("Spring river flower moon night"), in Tan Wuchang (ed.), *zhong guo xin shi bai pi shu: 1999–2002* (*Chinese New Poetry White Paper: 1999–2002*). Beijing: Kunlun Publishing House, 2004, p. 386.

Chen, Kehua, *qian kan tou shi* (*Head-hunting Poems*). Taipei: Chiuko Publishing, 1995.

Chen, Tieyuan, *liuxue & laji* (*Studying Overseas & Rubbish*). Beijing: World Knowledge Publishing House, 2004.

Chi, Li, *yu mou sha ren* (*A Pre-meditated Murder*). China Social Science Publishing House, 1993.

——, *lao wuhan: yong yuan de lang man* (*Old Wuhan: Always Romantic*). Jiangsu Fine Arts Publishing House, 2000.

Chin, Marilyn, in Ling-chi Wang and Yiheng Zhao, 1991, p. 30

Chinese Writers Association Creative Writing and Research Department (ed.), *2002 nian zhong guo shi ge jing xuan* (*A Selection of Chinese Poetry in 2002*). Wuhan: Changjiang Literature and Arts Publishing House, 2003.

ci hai (*Ocean of Words*). Shanghai: Shanghai Cishu Publishing House, 1981 [1977].

Clancy, Patricia and Allen, Jeanne (intro/trans.), *The French Consul's Wife: Memoirs of Céleste de Chabrillan in Gold-rush Australia*. Melbourne: Melbourne University Press, 1998.

Chinese-English Dictionary, A, 1982

Chung Wai Literary Monthly, Vol., 29, No. 3, August 2000.

Conlon, R.J., "The truth about yanks", *Overland*, No. 169, 2002, p. 69.

Cope, Bill and Kalantzis, Mary, *A Place in the Sun*. Sydney: HarperCollins, 2000.

Cun Yi, "*deng xiaoping gen ben mei you li lun*" ("Deng Xiaoping has no theory at all"), *China Monthly*, March 2001, p. 4.

Dai, Jinhua, *wu zhong feng jing: zhong guo dian ying wen hua: 1978–1998*. (*Scenery in a fog: Chinese cinema culture: 1978–1998*). Beijing: Beijing University Publishing House, 2000.

Dale, David, *100 Things Everyone Needs to Know About Australia*. trans. by Li Qingrui and Zhang Yingbao. China Tourist Publishing House, 2000.

Davis, H. R., *Yunnan: link between India and Yangtze River*. (Chinese trans. by Li Antai, et al.). Kunming: Yunnan Education Press, 2001 [original version published in 1911].

dang dai liu xing yu (Popular Contemporary Language). China Society Publishing House, 1999.

Dickens, Charles, *Oliver Twist*. London: Galley Press, 1987.

Du, Lengding, et al. (recorded), *zhong guo ren de yi ye qing* (*One Night Stand for Chinese People*). Hong Kong: Gong He Publishing House, 2003.

Duan, Peidong, *song shan da zhan* (*A Battle in Songshan Mountain*). Kunming: Yunnan People's Publishing House, 1995.

Duras, Marguerite, *Practicalities*. Flamingo, 1990 [1987].

Essay Overseas Edition. No. 4, 2000.

Fan Si, "*mei mei ni shi shui*" ("Sister you are water"), in Yang Ke (ed), *kaishi* (*Beginnings*). Fuzhou, China: Haifeng Publishing House, 2001, p. 230.

Fei, Chengkang, *zhong guo zu jie shi* (*A History of Foreign Settlements in China*). Shanghai: Shanghai Academy of Social Sciences, 1991.

Fei, Yong and Zhong, Xiaoyi, *gu long chuan qi* (*The Gu Long Legend*). Guangdong: Guangdong People's Publishing House, 1996.

——, *liang yu sheng chuan qi* (*The Liang Yusheng Legend*). Guangdong: Guangdong People's Publishing House, 1996.

The Folio Golden Treasury. London: the Folio Society, 1997.

Foster, E.M., *Aspects of the Novel*. Edward Arnold, 1974 [1927].

Fu, Lei, *fu lei jia shu* (*Fu Lei's Letters Home*). Beijing: Life, Reading, New Knowledge Three in One Bookshop, 1996.

Gao, Hongxing, *chan zu shi* (*A History of Foot-binding*). Shanghai Literature and Arts Publishing House, 1995.

Gao, Houman, *yue bu guo de ping zhang: zhong wai bian guan ji si mi lu* (*The Insurmountable Barrier: a secret record of anti-smuggling activities on the Chinese-foreign borders*). Beijing: PLA Press, 1995.

Gao, Xingjian, *yi ge ren de sheng jing* (*One Man's Bible*). Hong Kong: Cosmos Books, 2000.

Ge, Ahgan and He, Xiaodan, *wang guo zhi meng-gu pi de yu li jiang* (*Dream of the Kingdom – Peter Koo and Lijiang*). Kunming: Yunnan Education Press, 2000.

Genet, Jean, *The Thief's Journal*. Penguin, 1967 [1965].

Gilbert, Elizabeth, "Hollywood bust", *The Age* magazine *Good Weekend*, 19 August 2000, pp. 42–57.

Gizzi, Peter, "Rival", *Salt*, Vol. 15, 2002, p. 63.

Good Weekend (The Age Magazine), 17 March 2001; 23 June 2001; 18 August 2001; 24 November 2001.

Goldsworthy, Peter, "Winter Piece", in John Leonard (ed.), *Contemporary Australian Poetry*. Victoria: Houghton Mifflin Australia, 1990, p. 194.

Greer, Germaine, *The Female Eunuch*. London: HarperCollins, 1993 [1970].

——, *The Whole Woman*. New York: Alfred A. Knopf, 1999.

Griffiths, Tom, "Essaying the truth", *Meanjin*, No. 1, 2000, pp. 128–144.

Hamburger, Michael, "Introduction", in Paul Celan, *Poems of Paul Celan: revised and expanded* (trans. by Michael Hamburger). New York: Persea Books, Inc, 2002 [1972], pp. xix–xxxiv.

Hamner, Robert, "Divided in the Vein: Derek Walcott's Transcultural Translation", *Agenda*, Vol., 39, Nos. 1, 2, 3, winter, 2002–2003.

Han, Shaogong, *an shi* (*Insinuations*). Beijing: People's Literature Press, 2002.

han ying ci dian (*A Chinese-English Dictionary*), 1981 [1980].

Hauser, Ernest O, *Shanghai: City for Sale*. [translated in Chinese by Yue Yi in 1941]. Shanghai: Shanghai Bookshop Publishing House, 2000 [1940].

He, Jiangyu, and He, Laoyu, *gu du zhi lü-zhi wu xue jia, ren lei xue jia yue se fu luo ke he ta zai yun nan de tan xian jing li* (*The Lonely Journey: Joseph Rock as the botanist and anthropologist in his adventures in Yunnan*). Kunming: Yunnan Education Press, 2000.

Herbert, Xavier, *Capricornia*. Sydney: Angus and Robertson Publishers, 1985 [1938].

Herrick, Robert, Poem 103, *The Folio Golden Treasury*, chosen and introduced by James Michie. London: the Folio Society, 1997, p. 112.

Hong Ying, *ah nan* (*Ananda*). Changsha: Hunan Literature and Arts Publishing House, 2002.

——, *K*. Taipei: Er Ya Publishing House, 1999.

Huang Ai Dong Xi, *lao guang zhou* (*The Old Guangzhou*). Nanjing, Jiangsu: Jiangsu Fine Arts Publishing House, 1999.

Huang, Canran, *shi jie de yin yu* (*The Metaphor of the World*). Culture and Arts Publishing House, 1998.

Huang, Jie, *ren she: zhong guo tou du chao da zhui zong* (*The Human Snakes: a great pursuit of Chinese smuggling waves*). Hong Kong: Cosmos Books, 2002.

Huang, Wanhua, *wen hua zhuan huan zhong de shi jie hua wen wen xue* (*The Chinese Literature of the World in a Cultural Transition*). China Social Sciences Publishing House, 1999.

——, *xin ma bai nian hua wen xiao shuo shi* (*A Hundred-year History of Chinese-language Fiction in Singapore and Malaysia*). Shandong Literature and Arts Publishing House, 1999.

Hughes, Robert, *The Shock of the New*. Thames and Hudson, 1996 [1980].

Huntley-Badger, Luke, "The indefinable poem", in *JAAM*, May 2001, p. 160.

Isumo, Marou, *Love upon the Chopping Board*. Melbourne: Spinifex, 2000.

Jaivin, Linda, *The Monkey and the Dragon: a true story about friendship, music, politics and life on the edge*. Melbourne: Text Publishing, 2001.

Jia, Pingwa, *fei du* (*The Capital in Ruins*). Beijing: Beijing Publishing House, 1993.

Jiang, Mu, *zuo jia hua bian* (*Anecdotes about Writers*). Taipei: Vastplain Publishing House, 2000.

Jin, Mei, *fu lei zhuan* (*A Biography of Fu Lei*). Changsha, Hunan: Hunan Literature and Arts Publishing House, 1993.

jin shan yue kan (*Gold Mountain Monthly*), No. 10, 1999, p. 31; No. 12, 1999, p. 27.

Kauffmann, Jean-Paul (trans. by Patricia Clancy), *The Dark Room at Longwood: a voyage to St Helena*. London: Harville Press, 1999.

Jose, Nicholas, *Black Sheep: journey to Borroloola*. Vic: Hardie Grant Books, 2002.

Kennedy, Michael, *The Oxford Dictionary of Music* (new edition), Oxford: OUP, 1994.

King, Stephen, *On Writing: A Memoir of the Craft*. London: Hodder and Stoughton, 2000.

King, Zoe, "Zoe King talks to 'Scottish Poet' Kenneth Steven", in *BuzzWords*, 12, June 2000, p. 44.

Kinsella, John, "A loss of poetics", in *Agenda*, Vol., 39, No., 4, Summer, 2003, p. 259.

Kong, Qingmao, *lin shu zhuan* (*A Biography of Lin Shu*). Beijing: Tuanjie Publishing House, 1998.

Kuo, Alex, "Coming home", in Ling-chi Wang and Yiheng Zhao, 1991, p. 62.

Kundera, Milan, *bei bei pan de yi zhu* (*Les Testaments Trahis*). Shanghai: Oxford University Press and Shanghai People's Publishing House, 1995.

Lamu Gatusa, *meng huan lu gu hu-zui hou yi ge mu xing wang guo zhi mi* (*The Dreamlike Lugu Lake: the mystery of the last kingdom of women*). Kunming: Yunnan Fine Arts Publishing House, 1996.

Lao, Wei, *piao bo: bian yuan ren cai fang lu* (*Drifting: Interviews with People on the Edge*). China Play Publishing House, 1999.

Larkin, Philip, *Collected Poems*. Edited with an introduction by Anthony Thwaite. The Marvell Press and Faber and Faber, 1988.

Lawlor, Laurie, *Where will this shoe take you? A walk through the history of footwear*. New York: Walker and Company, 1996.

Lea, Bronwyn, "Poems for Seferis", *Salt*, Vol. 15, 2002, p.114.

——, "Cheap red wine", *Overland*, No. 166, 2002, p. 54.

Li, Biyu, *wang ming yi bang: mian gong you ji dui shi nian qin li ji* (*Exiled in an Alien Country: a factual account of my ten years in the Burmese Communist Guerrila*). Beijing: Beijing Shiyue Literature and Arts Publishing House, 2001.

Li, Mengsheng, *zhong guo jin hui xiao shuo bai hua* (*A Hundred Banned and Destroyed Books in China*). Shanghai: Shanghai Classics Publishing House, 1994.

Li, Shiyu, "*jia yi gong shang*" ("Let's appreciate good translation together"), in *Mingpo Monthly*, No. 1, 1999, pp. 125–126.

Li, Tuo, "*wen zi de zun yan*" ("The dignity of words"), in *Tianya* (Frontiers), No. 5, 1999, p. 22.

Lin, Mohan and Wei, Wei (eds), *women tuo chi na zhong zhong guo ren* (*We Despise That Kind of Chinese*). Gansu People's Publishing House, 1999.

Lin, Taiyi, *lin yu tang zhuan* (*A Biography of Lin Yutang*). Beijing: China Theatre Publishing House, 1994.

Ling, Dingnian, *shu xiang xiao zha* (*A Small Bunch of Book Fragrance*). Beijing: Beijing Yanshan Publishing House, 2002.

Li, Ya, *da lu de wen rou yi xiang* (*The Tender Otherland of the Mainland*). Taipei: Golden Rich International Ltd, 2001.

Lin, Yefu, *sui yue de chang he* (*The Long River of Years*). Penerbitan Meng Tian, 1999.

Ling, Yue, "At night, we stopped" (trans. by Ouyang Yu), in, *Otherland*, No., 8, 2002, special edition, titled, *In Your Face: Contemporary Chinese Poetry in English Translation*. Kingsbury, Australia: Otherland Publishing, p. 42.

Liu, E, *lao can you ji* (*The Travels of Old Can*). Taipei, 2000 [1976] (written in 1904).

Liu, Deqing, *ouyang xiu zhuan* (*A Biography of Ouyang Xiu*). Harbin: Harbin Publishing House, 1995.

Liu, Shaotang, *tu zhu ren sheng* (*Writing Life with Earth*). Shanghai: Shanghai Literature and Arts Publishing House, 1998.

Liu, Xiaobo, "*chen yin ke de ren ge*" ("Chen Yinke's personality"). *Ming Po Monthly*. December 2002, p. 47.

Liu, Yanyan, "*bu guo ru ci*" ("Just so so"), in *dajia* (OM), No. 5, 1999, p. 7.

Lodge, David, *mei hao de gong zuo* (*Nice Work*), trans. by Luo Yiyong, Beijing: Writers' Publishing House, 1998.

Lomer, Kathryn, "After the moon walk", *Imago*, Vol., 13, No., 3, 2001, p. 132.

Lu, Gusun (ed.), *The English Chinese Dictionary* (Unabridged). Shanghai: Shanghai Yiwen Publishing House, 1993.

Lu, Qiutian, *cha yi: yi wei zhong guo da shi yan zhong de dong xi fang si wei* (*The Difference: Eastern and Western ways of thinking in the eyes of a Chinese ambassador*). Shanghai: Shanghai Sanlian Bookshop Press, 2003.

Luo Fu, *xue beng: luo fu shi xuan* (*Avalanche: A Collection of Luo Fu's Poetry*). Bookman Books Publishing, Taiwan, 1994.

Luo, Xi, "*xin renlei zhong jian liu xing guai guai de yu*" ("Strange expressions popular among the new mankind"), in *Australian-Chinese Weekly*, 03/02/00, p. 19.

Ma, Jian, *Red Dust: a path through China*, translated into English by Flora Drew. New York: Anchor Books, 2002.

Ma, Jigao, and Huang, Jun, *zhong guo gu dai wen xue shi* (*A History of Ancient Chinese Literature*) (Vol. 3). Changsha, Hunan: Hunan Literature and Arts Publishing House, 1992.

Ma, Shuo, *he nan ren re shui le* (*Who did Henan People Upset?*). Haikou: Hainan Publishing House, 2002.

MacGowan, J., *zhong guo ren sheng huo de ming yu an* (*Men and Manners of Modern China*), translated by Zhu Tao and Ni Jing. Beijing: Current Affairs Publishing House, 1998 [1912].

Mai, Di (ed), *nan ren bu huai, nü ren bu ai* (*If a Man Isn't Bad, a Woman doesn't Love Him*). China International Broadcasting Publishing House, 1999.

Maugham, Somerset, *The Summing Up*. The New American Library: 1951 [1946].

Mews, Constance J., (trans. by Neville Chiavaroli and Constant J. Mews), *The Lost Love Letters of Heloise and Aberlard: perceptions of dialogue in twelfth-century France.* New York: St Martin's Press, 1999.

Mian Mian, *tang* (*Candy*). Beijing: China Play Publishing House, 2000.

Mu Zi Mei, *yi qing shu* (*Abandoned Love Letters*). Hong Kong: Cosmos Books, 2004.

nan fang zhou mo (*The Southern Weekend*), 1999.

Neilson, John Shaw, "The crane is my neighbour", in Ann Fairbairn (ed.), *Sunlines: an anthology of poetry to celebrate Australia's harmony in diversity.* Canberra: The Department of Immigration and Multicultural and Indigenous Affairs, pp. 24–25.

Ng, Lilian, *Swallowing Clouds.* Penguin, 1997.

Nisbet, Jennifer, "Literary time bomb", *Newswrite*, 3 February 2003, Issue 123, p. 3.

Nordbrandt, Henrik, "Offshore wind", *Salt*, Vol, 15, 2002, p. 182.

Oliver, Stephen, *Unmanned.* Wellington, New Zealand. HeadworX Publishers, 1999.

Otherland, No. 3, 1997.

Ouyang, Yu, "zhi jing" ("The Pinnacle"), *xiang gang wen xue* (Hong Kong Literature), No., 149, 1/5/1997, p. 71.

——, *Moon over Melbourne and Other Poems.* Melbourne: Papyrus Publishing, 1995.

——, "zhi wu ren" ("The Plant People"), *Otherland* (Yuanxiang), No. 3, 1997, pp. 73–4.

Overland, No. 158, 2000.

Shen, Minte, and Fang, Guorong (eds), *jiang nan wei dao* (*Tastes of South of the River*), Vol., 2. Haikou: Nanfang Publishing House, 1999.

The Oxford Dictionary of Quotations. (revised edition), 1996.

Padilla, Mario Rene, "Mediation at the Plaza Puerta de Moros", in *Atlanta Review*, Spring-Summer, 2003, p. 20.

Pavic, Milorad, *ha za er ci dian* (*Le dictionnaire khazar*). Shanghai: Shanghai Translated Text Publishing House, 1998.

Pham Thi Hoai, *The Crystal Messenger.* South Melbourne, Vic: Hyland House Publishing Pty Ltd, 1997.

Phillips, Robert, "AUSLÄNDER", *The Boulevard*, Vol., 15, No. 3, Spring 2000, pp. 1–25.

Pinto, Fernao Mendes, *pu tao ya ren zai hua jian wen* (*Accounts of China by Portuguese* or *Antologia dos Viajantes Portugueses na China*), trans. from Portuguese into Chinese by Wang Suoying. Haikou: Hainan Publishing House, 1998.

"Pornographic ads. appearing on the 'Shenzhen Hotlines' on the internet" (Hulianwang '*shenzhen rexian*' zhandian juran chuxian seqing tiezi), *Guangzhou Daily*, 03/02/99.

Porter, Dorothy, "It's too hard to write good – I'd rather write bad", from the online magazine *Australian Humanities Review*, March 2000.

Prichard, Selwyn, *Lunar Frost*. Sydney: Brandl & Schlesinger, 2000.

Qian, Liqun, "zhao hui shi luo de wen xue shi jie" ("Finding back the lost literary world"), in *Southern Literary Forum*, No. 5, 1999, p. 22.

Quintana, Anton (trans. by John Nieuwenhuizen), *The Baboon King*. St Leonards, NSW: Allen & Unwin, 1998.

Qing Yan (ed.), *li dai shi hua xiao pin* (*shi hua and xiao pin of Various Dynasties*). Hubei Lexicographical Work Publishing House, 1994.

Qiu, Huadong, *ku de yi dai* (*The Cool Generation*). Beijing: China Theatre Publishing House, 1999, p. 170.

Rao, Pengzi (ed), *zhong guo wen xue zai dong nan ya* (*Chinese Literature in South-east Asia*). Jinan: Jinan University Publishing House, 1999.

——, *xin ying* (*Shadows of the Heart*). Guangzhou: Huacheng Publishing House, 1995.

Scott, L.E., *Earth Colours*. Wellington: Headwork Publishers, 2000.

Shen, Haobo, "dian guang shi huo de peng zhuang" ("The clashes between the electric light and the stone fire"), in *shi can kao* (*Poem Reference* [original title]), October, 1999, pp. 186–187.

——, *xin cang da e* (*Great Evil Hidden in the Heart*). Dalian: Dalian Publishing House, 2004 [this book banned subsequently].

Shen, Zhi, and Zheng, Xiaolin (eds), *quan guo shan he yi pian "hong"* (*A Spread of "Red" in the Whole Country*). Beijing: Unity Publishing House, 1993.

Shi, Kang, *yi ta hu tu* (*A Total Mess*). Beijing: Minzu Publishing House, 2001.

Shi, Shengtai, *ren ke mao xiang: qi ye guan ren shu* (*You Can Measure One's Face: the skill of observing people in business*). Shibao Publishing, 1997.

Shi, Xiaojun, "The North" (translated by Ouyang Yu), *Imago*, Vol., 9, No. 3, 1997, p. 111.

shu cheng (*Reading* [original title]), No. 11, 1999, p. 25 and p. 48.

Shu, Xincheng, *jin dai zhong guo liu xue shi* (*A History of Chinese Students Overseas in Modern Times*). Hong Kong: China Books Bureau, 1989 [1926].

Sima, Jinlin (ed), *sheng huo zhen han: tou shi zhong guo da an* (*Life Shocks: X-raying China's Big Crime Cases*). Inner Mongolia Publishing House, 1998.

Song, Xiaoxian, "1958", in Yang Ke (ed) *kai shi* (*Beginnings*). Fuzhou, China: Haifeng Publishing House, 2001, p. 35.

Song, Yiqiao, *zui qiu zhong ji de ling hun: xu di shan zhuan* (*Pursuing the Ultimate Soul: a biography of Xu Dishan*). Fuzhou, Fujian: Haixia Literature and Arts Publishing House, 1989.

Su, Yang, *wen tan qing hong bang* (*The Black and Red Gangs in the World of Letters*). Beijing: Culture and Arts Publishing House, 2001.

Syson, Ian, "Muscling in", *Overland*, No. 166, 2002, p. 2.

Szymborska, Wistawa, *Poems New and Collected: 1957–1997*. [trans. Stanislaw Baranczak and Clare Cavanagh]. Harcourt, Inc., 1998.

Tadié, Yves, *La critique littérraire au XXèmee siècle*, translated by Shi Zhongyi and published by Baihua Literature and Arts Publishing House, 1998.

Tang, Yangzong, "*fang lin*" ("Fragrant Neighbour"), in *2003 nian wen xue jing pin: shi ge juan* (*Fine Literary Works in 2003: the poetry volume*) [Ed. Han Zuorong]. Beijing: People's Publishing House, 2004, p. 123.

Tao, Muning, *qing lou wen xue yu zhong guo wen hua* (*Literature of Green Mansions and Chinese Culture*). Dongfang Publishing House, 1993.

Teng, Bin, "pu tian le" ("Celebration Everywhere"), in Zhu Binjie (ed), *san bai shou xiang zhu yuan qu (300 Yuan Dynasty Qu-poems with Detailed Notations)*. Nanchang: Baihuazhou Literature and Arts Publishing House, 1995, p. 108.

Thomev, Jim (selected/translated), *Small Tales, Great Wisdom: Macedonian sayings and fables exercises in the art of astonishment.* Queenscliff, Vic.: Black on White Publications, 1999.

Third Rock from the Sun. American TV drama. Broadcast on Channel 8 in 2000.

Tian Dao and Nan Ba (eds/co-write), *wen ren de duan qiao* (*The Broken Bridge of Men of Letters*). Guangming Daily Publishing House, 1997.

Tuohy, Wendy, "Love in a corporate climate", *The Age*, 26/7/03 (Sat), p. 3.

tianya (*Frontiers*), No. 5, 1999, p. 117.

Time, February 21, 2000.

Vilar, Esther (trans. by Udo Borgert and Laura Ginters), *Timetable of Revenge* (unpublished play). 1997.

Waldersee, Alfred Heinrich Karl Ludwig Count von, *A Field-marshal's Memoirs*. [translated into Chinese by Wang Guangqi as *wa de xi quan luan bi ji* or *Waldersee Notes on the Boxers' Rebellion*]. Shanghai: Shanghai Bookshop Publishing House, 1999 [1924].

Walker, David, *Anxious Nation: Australia and the Rise of Asia 1850–1939*. St Lucia: UQP, 1999.

Wang, Anna, *xin huai nan ren de shi dai* (*The Age of the New Bad Men*). Jilin People's Publishing House, 1999, p. 150.

Wang, Guofu, (ed/trans), *Macquarie English-Chinese Dictionary*. Suzhou: Suzhou University Press, 1999.

Wang, Hongxu, *di san zi yan jing tou shi jing cheng* (*The Third Eye X-raying Beijing*). China Theatre Publishing House, 1999.

Wang, Jiaxin, *you dong xuan ya* (*The Drifting Cliffs*). Hunan Literature and Arts Publishing House, 1997.

Wang, Jinjun, *beijing ao yun 2008* (*The 2008 Olympic Games in Beijing*). Beijing: Authors Publishing House, 2001.

Wang, Ling-chi, and Henry Yiheng Zhao (eds), *Chinese American Poetry: An Anthology*. Asian American Voices, 1991.

Wang, Shaoxi, *xiao qie shi* (*A History of Concubines*). Shanghai Literature and Arts Publishing House, 1995.

Wang, Shunjian, "wang shi shi zhong hui zhao shang men lai" ('Things of the past will always find their way to your door"), in Yang Ke (ed), *kai shi* (*Beginnings*). Fuzhou, China: Haifeng Publishing House, 2001, p. 5.

Wang, Weizhi (ed), *zai xiang xiang yu xian shi zhi jian zuo suo: chen li zuo pin ping lun ji* (*Walking the Line Between the Imagination and the Reality: a collection of critical articles on Chen Li*). Taiwan: Bookman Press, 1999.

Wang, Xiaobo, *chen mo de da duo shu* (*Silence of the Majority*). Beijing: China Youth Publishing House, 1997.

Watanabe, Junichi, *shi le yuan* (*Paradise Lost*), trans. Tan Ling. Beijing: Culture and Arts Publishing House and Cosmos Books, 1998.

Weale, Putnam, *Indiscreet Letters from Peking,* translated by Leng Tai and Chen Yixian as *gen zi shi guan bei wei ji* (*An account of how the embassies were besieged by the Boxers*). Shanghai: Shanghai Bookshop Publishing, 1999 [1917].

Wei Hui, *shanghai bao bei* (*Shanghai Baby*). Shenyang, Liaoning: Chunfeng Literature and Arts Publishing House, 1999.

Wilding, Michael, "The brave new world of publishing", *Newswrite* (The monthly magazine of the NSW Writers' Centre), No. 111, Dec 01/Jan 02, 2001–2002, p. 3.

Window, Carolin, *Dim*. Random House Australia Pty Ltd, 1996.

Xi Du, *ge mai shi quan bian* (*Complete Collection of Ge Mai's Poems*). Shanghai: Shanghai Sanlian Sudian, 1999.

Xia Tian *(ed), zhong guo da min yao (Great Chinese Folk Rhymes)*. Hong Kong: Cosmos Books Ltd, 2000.

Xia, Xinhai, *zhong guo de tao tie* (*Gluttons in China*). Zhuhai: Zhuhai Publishing House, 1997.

xian dai han yu ci dian (*Modern Chinese Dictionary*). Beijing: Shangwu Yinshu Guan, 1978.

Xiao An, "*sheng huo de mi mi*" ("Secrets of life"), *1998 zhong guo xin shi nian jian* (*China New Poem Almanac 1998*), ed. by Yang Ke. Huacheng Publishing House, 1999, p. 220.

xianggang wenhui (Hong Kong P.E.N.), March, 2000.

xin ying han ci dian (*A New English-Chinese Dictionary*), 1981 [1978].

Xu, Chengbei, *lao beijing* (*The Old Beijing*). Nanjing, Jiangsu: Jiangsu Fine Arts Publishing House, 1999.

Xu Xi, *The Unwalled City, a Novel of Hong Kong*. Hong Kong: Chameleon Press Ltd, 2001.

Xu, Yong, "*zu lan*" ("The bamboo basket"), in Zang Di and Xi Du (eds), *bei da shi xuan: 1978–1998* (*A Selection of Poetry at Beijing University: 1978–1998*). China Literature Publishing House, 1998, p. 115.

Yan, Li, Yi Sha and Ma Fei, *yi hang cheng san* (*One Line by Three*). Qinghai People's Publishing House, 1995.

Yang, Bo, *zui e de yi dian yuan* (*The Sinful Garden of Eden*). China Society Publishing House, 1998.

Yang, Hai, and Xu, Jun, *ji nü shi* (*A History of Prostitutes*). Shanghai Literature and Arts Publishing House, 1995.

Yang, Ke, *zhong guo xin shi nian jian 2002–2003* (*China New Poem Almanac 2002–2003*). Tianjin: Tianjin Social Sciences Academy Publishing House, 2003, p. 557.

Yang, Ping, *chu jing* (*Situation*). Taipei: Tonshan Publishing House, 2003.

Yang, Xiaolin, *yun nan bai nian gu shi* (*A Hundred-year Story of Yunnan*). Kunming: Yunnan People's Publishing House, 2001.

Yao, Chaowen, *hua wen wei pian xiao shuo xue yuan li yu chuang zuo* (*Principles and Creative Writing in the Studies of Overseas Chinese Micro-fiction*). Beijing: China Wenlian Press, 2002.

Yi Fu, *meng xing ao da li ya* (*Woken up from the dream in Australia*), China Workers' Publishing House, 1995.

Yi Sha, *er shi shi ren* (*Starving the poets*). Beijing: China Overseas Chinese Press, 1994.

——, *yi ge dou bu fang guo* (*Won't Let Go of a Single One*). Xining: Qinghai People's Press, 1999.

ying han da ci dian (*The English-Chinese Dictionary*) [unabridged] , 1995 [1993].

Yu, Jian, "qi shi, ta xie yi bu jiu gou le" ("In fact, it's enough for him to write one book"), *yue du dao kan* (*Reading Report*), No. 3, 1999, p. 7.

Yu, Xiang, "suo yi ni ai wo" ("So you love me"), in Yang Ke (ed.), *2001 zhong guo xin shi nian jian* (*China New Poem Almanac 2001*). Haifeng Publishing House: Guangdong, 2002, p. 3.

Yu, Zhi, *mo deng shang hai* (*Modern Shanghai*). Shanghai: Shanghai Bookshop Press, 2003.

Yuan, Hongdao, *yuan zhong lang sui bi* (*Essays by Yuan Zhonglang*). Beijing: The Authors' Press, 1995.

Zang, Di and Xi Du (eds), *bei da shi xuan: 1978–1998* (*A selection of poetry at Beijing University: 1978–1998*). Beijing: China Literature Publishing House, 1998.

Zephaniah, Benjamin, *Propa Propaganda*. Bloodaxe Books, 1996.

Zhang, Chunfan, *jiu wei gui* (*The Nine-tailed Turtle*) (3 volumes). Beijing: People's China Publishing House, 1993.

Zhang, Longxi, "dao de you xiang qi ma?" ("Does morality carry fragrance?"), in *Essay Overseas Edition* (*sanwen haiwai ban*), No. 3, 2000, pp. 28–29.

Zhang, Minhua, "Daily life" (a poem), *Otherland*, No. 8, 2001.

Zhang, Yudan, *yun nan shi ba guai xun zong* (*Tracking "The Eighteen Oddities" in Yunnan*). Kunming: Yunnan People's Publishing House, 1999.

Zhang, Zao, *chun qiu lai xin* (*Spring and Autumn Letters*). Culture and Arts Publishing House, 1998.

Zhang, Zhenhai, *xin xin ren lei* (*The New New Generation*). Beijing: China Industrial and Commercial United Publishing House, 1999.

Zhang, Zhongxian (wrote/ed), *zhong guo da lü shi bian hu shi lu* (*A Record of Defence Cases by Barristers in China*), Beijing: Jincheng Publishing House, 1997.

Zhao, Chuan, *hai wai•ren* (*Overseas•People*). Shanghai: Shanghai Bookshop Publishing House, 2000.

Zhao, Changtian, *gu du de wai lai zhe – da qing hai guan zong shui wu si he de* (*The Lonely Outsider: Hart, Chief Customs Taxation Officer in the Great Qing Dynasty*). Shanghai: Wenhui Publishing House, 2003.

Zhao, Chuan, *yuan yang hu die* (*Mandarin Ducks and Butterflies*). Taipei: Unitas Publishing Co. Ltd, 2003.

Zhao, Dong (ed), *zao yu yang hun* (*Encountering Foreign Marriages*). Zhengzhou: Henan People's Publishing House, 2000.

Zhao, Henry Yiheng, *dang shuo zhe bei shuo de shi hou* (*When the Sayer is Said*). Beijing: China People's University, 1998.

Zhao, Leslie (see Zhao Chuan).

Zhao, Liangjun, (directed), *jin ji* (*Golden Rooster*), a film made in 2002.

Zhao, Ning, *li hun shi dai* (*The Age of Divorce*). Nanjing: Jiangsu Literature and Arts Publishing House, 2001.

Zheng, Ling, "xing cun ze" ("The survivor"), in Yang Ke (ed.), *2001 zhong guo xin shi nian jian* (*China New Poem Almanac 2001*). Guangdong: Haifeng Publishing House, 2002, p. 200.

Zhong Dao, "Days", "Giving up on the past" and "Man is floating on the rivers and lakes". See *shi can kao* (*Poem Reference*), October, 1999, pp. 149–151.

——(ed.), *shi can kao* (*Poem Reference*). No. 16, July, 2000.

zhong guo wen hua bao (*The Chinese Culture Daily*), 1 April, 1999, p. 4.

Zhou, Lunyou, "xuan bu xi fang zhong xin hua yu quan li wu xiao: guan yu jian li 'xian dai de zhong guo ben tu wen xue' de si kao ti gang" ("Announcing the invalidity of the power of the Western-centred discourse: on the thought-outline of establishing 'a modern local Chinese literature'"), from *han yu wen xue* (*Chinese-language Literature*) [online Chinese magazine], No. 1, 2000.

Zhou, Zuoren, *zhi tang xiao pin* (*Xiao-ping Essays from Hall of Knowledge*). Shanxi People's Publishing House, 1991.

Zhu, Binjie (ed), *san bai shou xiang zhu yuan qu* (*300 Yuan Dynasty Qu-poems with Detailed Notations*). Nanchang City: Baihuazhou Literature and Arts Publishing House, 1995.

Zhu, Dake, *gua zao de shi dai: zai hua ye he xin nian de xian chang* (*The Noisy Age: at the site of the discourse and faith*). Hunan Literature and Arts Publishing House, 1998.

——, Wu Xuan, Xu Jiang, Qin Bazi, et al, *shi zuo jia pi pan* (*Critique of Ten Authors*). Shanxi Normal University Publishing House, 1999.

Zhu, Jian and Wang, Chaoguang, *min guo ying tan* (*The Cinema in the Republic of China*). Jiangsu Ancient Books Publishing House, 1997.

Zhu, Luzi and Yang, Aixiang, *zou huo ru mo de ying yu* (*The Devilishly Possessed English*). Changsha: Hunan People's Publishing House, 2004.

Zhu, Wen, *wo ai mei yuan* (*I Love American Dollars*). Beijing: Authors' Publishing House, 1995.

Zi Ping (ed.), *zhong gong gao guan se qing dang an* (*The Pornographic Files of High Officials of the Chinese Communists*). Hong Kong: Xiafei'er International Publishing Company, 1999.

——(ed.), *zhong gong da yin guan* (*The Big Obscene Officials of the Chinese Communists*). Hong Kong: Xiafei'er International Publishing Company, 2000.

zi li kuai bao (The Independence Daily), 18/6/96, p.2; 20/6/96, p.1.

Wakefield Press is an independent publishing and
distribution company based in Adelaide, South Australia.
We love good stories and publish beautiful books.
To see our full range of titles, please visit our website at
www.wakefieldpress.com.au.